Nitty-Gritty Grammar

Nitty-Gritty Grammar

A Not-So-Serious Guide to Clear Communication

Edith H. Fine and Judith P. Josephson

TEN SPEED PRESS
Berkeley

Library of Congress Cataloging-in-Publication Data
Fine, Edith Hope.
    Nitty-gritty grammar / by Edith H. Fine and Judith P. Josephson.
       p.   cm.
    Includes bibliographical references (p.) and index.
    1. English language--Grammar.   I. Josephson, Judith Pinkerton.
    II. Title.
PE1112.F53   1998
428.2--dc21   97-44240
                                                             CIP
ISBN: 978-0-89815-966-0 (alk. paper)

Printed in the United States of America

Cover and text design: Susan Van Horn

23 22 21 20 19 18

First Edition

*Our thanks to Julie Castiglia, our hardworking agent,
and Chelsea Vaughn, our intrepid editor.*

*Kudos to our excellent readers—Enid Norman, Hilary Crain, Janelle Fine,
Jill Hansen, Melissa Irick, Jeannie Phelan, Mary Pinkerton, and Kay Vaughan.*

To English teachers everywhere—bless them.

CONTENTS

Part I. Words at Work

Part II. Building Blocks

Part III. Punctuation Pointers

Part IV. Word Power

Introduction

"*Grammar*? You're kidding, right?"

We had been teaching writing workshops at San Diego State for several years when the Director of Extension Programs at the College of Extended Studies asked us to build a grammar review class. Her request baffled us. Who would come? What would keep people from nodding off? Would we need a brass band to liven up our six-hour workshop?

Then again, we *are* both nutty enough to have *liked* diagramming in school. As teachers, we've touted grammar and explained it to young children, teenagers, and adults. As writers, we constantly edit and proofread, ever on the lookout for grammar gaffes—scrutinizing manuscripts, menus, billboards, articles, and ads. We even offer a grammar service, called Goof-Proofers! Slam dunk! The class was a go.

First came a nonthreatening, practical title: *Nitty-Gritty Grammar*.

Second, we needed razzle-dazzle. Given that grammar is a *very* serious business, we naturally thought of cartoons. Knowing that a good belly laugh is worth twenty furrowed brows, we culled our vast collection to find great grammar cartoons. We knew that most people hadn't thought about grammar since high school; we'd ease them in with humor.

Third, we honed in on the basics—the structure beneath our often perplexing English language. Our first students helped guide us, with questions such as "What's a subject?" "Agreement?" "Aren't prepositions those three-letter words?" "How *do* you spell 'potato'?"

Over the years, we've taught a wonderfully eclectic mix of people—sales reps, parents, students, medical workers, lawyers, engineers, secretaries, retirees, teachers, social workers, human resource managers, reporters, people new to English, and many others. We always promise students two A's if they remember to spell "grammar" with two a's!

Class participants cite similar complaints—"My boss redlines my work!" "I never learned grammar in the first place," "Grammar's my downfall," "I listen to newscasters' mistakes, and then wonder about the rules!"

Before we knew it, friends, relatives, and students were sending us grammar pet peeves, puzzlers, and gems for our Blooper Patrol Handbook. This became the Ticker Tape that runs through this book at the bottom of the page.

Nitty Gritty Grammar: A Not-So-Serious Guide to Clear Communication is for people who want to speak and write well and who can't afford to have errors tarnish their image. This feet-on-the-ground guide is designed in short "sound bites"—perfect for reading while on a coffee break, stirring the stew, or waiting in the doctor's office. In just minutes a day, you can review grammar basics, spot common errors, and brush up on your skills.

We've designed this book to be funny, unintimidating, and clear. Popular cartoons illustrate key points. Look for the right way, the wrong way, and the "why" to help you conquer grammar pitfalls.

As you plunge into this refresher, remember our maxim: Basically, between you and I—whoops!—grammar is fun!

— Edith H. Fine and Judith P. Josephson
Encinitas, California
December 1997

PART I:
WORDS AT WORK

Words do specific jobs in sentences to create meaning.

Verbs are the engines that power sentences. Without a verb, a sentence goes nowhere. Verbs show action or express a state of being.

The train **sped** through the tunnel of love.
(action)

Paige **is** tired of TV dinners.
(state of being)

Nouns are namers. Nouns name persons, places, things, or ideas.

The **ballerina** thundered onto the **stage**.
(person)   *(thing)*

Pat's in **love.** She's off to **Venezuela**.
(idea)   *(place)*

Pronouns are substitutes. They take the place of nouns.

For . . .
Dumbo teetered on a high wire.
(noun)

You can substitute . . .
He teetered on a high wire.
(pronoun)

Prepositions are locators. Prepositions can show position or time. They can also compare or connect.

An angry bee buzzed **into** Jake's tuba.
(preposition)

Bridget went bungee-jumping **after** lunch.
(preposition)

e Taj Mahal is a **unique** building. (*Not*, **most unique** or **very unique**—see page 39.)

3

Adjectives are describers. They describe or modify nouns or other adjectives.

> The groom wore **plaid** sneakers with his tux.
> *(adjective)*

Adverbs are also describers. They modify verbs, telling *how, when, where, how much,* or *to what extent.*

> **Gently,** Louie coaxed the pig into its pen.
> *(adverb—how)*

> "Bring me my chocolate torte **now**!" yelled Prudence.
> *(adverb—when)*

> Superman zoomed **skyward.**
> *(adverb—where)*

Adverbs can also modify adjectives or other adverbs.

> The **very warm** airplane cabin made the sherbet melt.
> *(adverb) (adjective)*

> Mrs. Tether's wig slipped **slightly askew.**
> *(adverb) (adverb)*

Interjections are outsiders. They aren't official parts of a sentence. Interjections show feelings.

> **Well,** Tom Cruise just called.
> *(mild interjection)*

> **Gross**! Dad's cooking liver.
> *(strong interjection)*

Conjunctions are connectors. They join words or parts of a sentence.

> Bagels **and** lox taste great together.
> *(conjunction)*

> I won't date Harold **unless** he ditches that mustache.
> *(conjunction)*

They signed the card, "**The Smiths.**" (*Not*, "**The Smith's.**"—see page 60.)

Verbs

FOR BETTER OR FOR WORSE by Lynn Johnston

Verbs are the engines that power sentences. Every complete sentence needs a verb.

Verbs can show **action**.

fly	soar	stagger	tattle
sail	spend	stomp	whisper

Snakes **slither** through slippery grass.
(verb)

Other verbs indicate a **state of being**. They are forms of the verb "be": *am, is, are, was, were, has been, will be.*

Dracula **is** a vampire.
(verb)

Some verbs are **helping verbs**. They work together with other verbs. Forms of "be" are often helping verbs. Other helping verbs are *has, have, had, can, could, will, would, shall, should, may, might.* (See page 7.)

can graduate   **have** decoded   **will have** flown
(helping verb)   *(helping verb)*   *(helping verb)*

Other verbs link ideas. See appendix, page 92, for examples of **linking verbs**.

A number of tickets **are** available. (*Not,* **A number** . . . *is*—see pages 87–88.)

5

INFINITIVES

An infinitive is the base form of a verb plus the word "to"—as in "to play." Use the infinitive form to test whether or not a word is a verb. Put "to" in front of the word that you think is a verb. If the "to" form suggests action, the word is a verb. These pairs work:

<table>
<tr><td>to hike
(verb)</td><td>to hover
(verb)</td><td>to help
(verb)</td></tr>
</table>

If the "to" form creates a mismatch, the word is not a verb. These don't work. They're not verbs:

<table>
<tr><td>to elephant
(noun)</td><td>to elegant
(adjective)</td><td>to exactly
(adverb)</td></tr>
</table>

When words fall between "to" and a verb, they split the infinitive. Until recently, "Don't split infinitives" was a hard-and-fast rule.

Split infinitive:	The fix:
to **quickly** *run*	*to* *run* **quickly**
to **once again** *thank you*	*to* *thank you* **once again**

CROCK by Bill Rechin and Don Wilder

Although the rule is changing, avoid splitting the infinitive when possible. If fixing the split infinitive makes the words sound awkward, skip it. The grammar patrol won't get you. Witness *Star Trek*'s famous line:

" . . . *to* **boldly** *go* where no one has gone before."

With infinitive phrases, avoid substituting "and" for "to." For example, "Look *to* see if you have my keys," *not* "Look *and* see if you have my keys."

Carlin **brought** cookies to our party. (*Not*, **brang**—see page 95.)

VERB TENSES

ABY BLUES by Rick Kirkman and Jerry Scott

Besides highlighting verb tenses, this *Baby Blues* cartoon also covers pronouns. (See page 17.) The busy mom should say, "*She* has a ball."

Verbs have different tenses. Time makes the difference. Verbs change form depending on when the action takes place—the present, the past, the future, or somewhere in between. Here are the three main tenses:

(Present Tense)	(Past Tense)	(Future Tense)
Today	**Yesterday**	**Tomorrow**
I dance.	I danced.	I will dance.

With helping verbs, you can create three other tenses for an event that takes place before or after another event. The "perfect" tenses always take helping verbs. Form the present perfect with "have" or "has." Form the past perfect with "had." Think of the past perfect as the "deep past." Form the future perfect with "will have" or "shall have."

(Present Perfect Tense)	(Past Perfect Tense)	(Future Perfect Tense)
Today	**Yesterday**	**Tomorrow**
I have danced.	I had danced.	I will have danced.

Bill **has painted** the kitchen hot pink.
   (*present perfect*)

Christine **will call** when she **reaches** Stratford.
   (*future*)   (*present*)

He **had eaten** sauerkraut before he **kissed** her.
   (*past perfect*)   (*past*)

By May, the next space shuttle **will have flown**.
   (*future perfect*)

Terry's **happier** now (or **more happy**). (*Not,* **more happier**—see page 39.)

Present Tense

The present tense shows action taking place today—"now." Verbs in the present tense change form depending on *who* is doing the action. Most verbs are **regular**—they follow a regular pattern. The verbs "walk" and "search" are regular.

Singular		Plural	
First Person I	**I walk** **I search**	*First Person* we	**we walk** **we search**
Second Person you	**you walk** **you search**	*Second Person* you	**you walk** **you search**
Third Person he, she, it	**he/she/it** *walks* **he/she/it** *searches*	*Third Person* they	**they walk** **they search**

TIP: To form the third-person singular of regular verbs, add *s* or *es* in the present tense.

He winks.   She smooches.   Love blossoms.

Right
She **moves** like a cheetah. He **moves** like a tortoise.

Wrong
She **move** like a cheetah. He **move** like a tortoise.

? **Why?**
With regular verbs, such as "move," add *s* or *es* to the base form in the third-person singular.

A **series** of storms **is coming.** (*Not*, **series . . . are coming**—see page 15.)

Irregular Verbs

Some verbs are **irregular**. Here is the present tense of the irregular verb "be":

Singular		Plural	
First Person I	I *am*	*First Person* we	we *are*
Second Person you	you *are*	*Second Person* you	you *are*
Third Person he, she, it	he, she, or it *is*	*Third Person* they	they *are*

PARTICIPLES

A participle is a verb form. Participles of regular verbs end with *ing* for the present tense and *d* or *ed* for the past tense.

boil	scatter	dazzle	stop	dash
boiling	scattering	dazzling	stopping	dashing
boiled	scattered	dazzled	stopped	dashed

Past Tense and Past Perfect Tense

The past tense shows action that has already taken place. With **regular** verbs, form the past tense and the past participle by adding *d* or *ed* to the present (base) form. Use the helping verb "had" with the participle to form the past perfect. "Had" shows action that was completed before another action took place.

Past: Jane's clients **returned** year after year.
Past Perfect: Paul **had framed** Kathleen's awards.

Examples of Regular Verb Forms

Present (base form)	Past	Past Perfect (past participle plus helping verb)
move	moved	had moved
iron	ironed	had ironed
trail	trailed	had trailed

The company relies **on Anne and me**. (*Not*, on Anne and myself—see page 24.)

Irregular verbs have different forms for the past and the past participle. They don't follow the pattern of regular verbs that form the past participle by just adding *d* or *ed*. (See appendix, pages 95–96, for a list of more irregular verbs.)

Examples of Irregular Verb Forms

Present (base form)	*Past*	*Past Perfect* (past participle plus helping verb)
do	did	had done
go	went	had gone
give	gave	had given
swim	swam	had swum

I **go** to karate today.
(*present*)

I **went** to karate yesterday.
(*past*)

I **had gone** to karate until last January.
(*past perfect*)

Right
Captain Hook **had swum** faster than the crocodile.
(*helping verb with past participle*)

Wrong
Captain Hook **had swam** faster than the crocodile.
(*helping verb with past verb form*)

? **Why?** The past participle "swum" teams with the helping verb "had"—"had swum." "Swam" is the past form. It stands alone: Captain Hook *swam* faster than the crocodile.

Future Tense

The future tense shows action that will take place in the future. Use "will" or "shall" and the present (base) form of the verb for the future tense. Use "will have" or "shall have" and the participle for the future perfect.

Future: Rhona **will learn** a seventh language.
Future Perfect: By Tuesday, Kitty **will have finished** her cookbook.

I see **him and me** getting married. (*Not*, **he and I**—see page 22.)

10

SUBJECT-VERB AGREEMENT

Verbs must agree with their subjects. Make subjects and verbs match in both person (I, you, he/she/it, we, you, they) and number (singular or plural). (See page 14 for an explanation of number.)

Person:
Say, "**He doesn't**," *not* "**He don't.**"
("Doesn't" is third person singular. "Doesn't" goes with *he, she,* and *it*.)

Number:
Say, "The **fire crackles**." ("It crackles," *not* "It crackle.")
    (singular noun) (singular verb)

Say, "The **embers glow**." ("They glow," *not* "They glows.")
    (plural noun) (plural verb)

Right
Vitamin **supplements improve** your love life.
    (plural noun)   *(plural verb)*

Wrong
Vitamin **supplements improves** your love life.
    (plural noun)   *(singular verb)*

? **Why?** The subject, "vitamin supplements," is plural. "Improve" is the plural form of the verb. To check the verb form, substitute the pronoun "they" for "supplements." Say, "They improve," not "They improves." (See page 8.)

Contractions such as "here's" or "there's" also cause agreement problems. "Here**'s** my **flip-flops**" really says, "Here **is** my **flip-flops**." Say, "Here **are** my **flip-flops**."

Right
There **are** only blue **jelly beans** left.
    (plural verb)   *(plural noun)*

Wrong
There**'s** only blue **jelly beans** left.
    (singular verb)   *(plural noun)*

? **Why?** "Jelly beans" is plural. Match it with a plural verb. Here, a singular verb is hidden in the contraction "there's"—"there is."

I hope it won't rain, Sam. (*Not,* **Hopefully**—see page 82.)

Subject-Verb Agreement with Prepositional Phrases

Prepositional phrases that come between the subject and the verb can be confusing. To check for subject-verb agreement, think of the sentence without the prepositional phrase. (Rusty on prepositions? See pages 31–33.)

Right
The **structure** of atoms **boggles** the mind.
   (singular noun)   *(singular verb)*

Wrong
The **structure** of atoms **boggle** the mind.
   (singular noun)   *(plural verb)*

? **Why?** "Of atoms" is a prepositional phrase. Don't let prepositional phrases trick you. Work with the subject and the verb only: "The structure . . . boggles."

Right
Weaknesses in the bond market **have surfaced.**
   (plural subject)   *(plural verb)*

Wrong
Weaknesses in the bond market **has surfaced.**
   (plural subject)   *(singular verb)*

? **Why?** The subject of the sentence, "weaknesses," is plural. Use a plural verb. Omit the prepositional phrase "in the bond market." Say, "Weaknesses have surfaced." (Or, "They have surfaced.")

ACTIVE VOICE AND PASSIVE VOICE

Verbs can be active or passive. Active verbs put the person or thing doing the action in charge. That's why newspaper headlines use the active voice. With the passive voice, the subject receives the action.

TIP: The prepositions "by," "to," or "for" can signal the passive voice.

Jay **passed** the marriage test.
   (active verb)

The marriage test **was passed** *by* Jay.
   (passive verb)

I **feel bad** about failing the test. (*Not*, **feel badly**—see pages 79–80.)

Active The Chicago Bulls **won** the game.

Passive The game **was won** *by* the Chicago Bulls.

Putting the "doer" in charge makes sentences stronger, shorter, and more direct.

While the active voice is stronger, it's often hard to avoid the passive voice in scientific, medical, or technical writing:

> The solution **was composed** of 25 ml of acetic acid and 100 ml of water.

The passive also puts the emphasis on the most important idea in the sentence. During a root canal, the comfort of the patient may be the most important idea:

> The patient **was given** laughing gas by Dr. Paine.

CALVIN AND HOBBES by Bill Watterson

English is constantly changing. Over time, other parts of speech can evolve into verbs. Today, these words double as nouns and verbs:

access   calendar   chair   film   input   parent

Avoid "verbing" non-verbs: to overnight, to office, to obsolete. (See page 6.)

Flo and I learned belly dancing. (*Not,* **Flo and me**—see page 17.)

Nouns

Nouns are namers. Nouns name persons, places, things, or ideas.

> **Archaeologists** found mammoth **bones** in the **quarry**.
> *(persons)*   *(things)*   *(place)*

> **Honesty** matters, but may not win **votes**.
> *(idea)*   *(things)*

Nouns can be common or proper. **Common nouns** name persons, places, things, or ideas. **Proper nouns** name *specific* persons, places, or things. Capitalize proper nouns.

> I leave for the **city** soon.
> *(common noun)*

> I leave for **Denver** soon.
> *(proper noun)*

> A **woman** ran the **country**.
> *(common noun)*   *(common noun)*

> **Indira Gandhi** ran **India**.
> *(proper noun)*   *(proper noun)*

One or More?

Singular means one. **Plural** means more than one. Nouns can be singular or plural: one dill *pickle*, seven dill *pickles*. Some nouns—such as *trousers, goods, scissors*—are always plural, even though they're a single object. (See page 67 for more on plural nouns.)

> My **trousers are** neon green.
> *(plural noun) (plural verb)*

Fabio **cannot** meet you for lunch. (*Not,* Fabio **can not**—see page 59.)

COLLECTIVE NOUNS

LLY FORTH by Greg Howard and Craig MacIntosh

Collective nouns stand for groups of persons, places, or things that act as units—words such as *team, corps, herd, flock, family, jury, crew, audience, assembly, band, faculty, nation, committee, class*. Collective nouns usually take **singular verbs**.

TIP: Substitute the word "it" for a collective noun to help you choose the right verb form.

Right

The **orchestra plays** classical and pop music.
  (collective noun) (singular verb)

Wrong

The **orchestra play** classical and pop music.
  (collective noun) (plural verb)

? **Why?** The collective noun "orchestra" takes a singular verb. "Plays" is the third person singular form of the verb. Say, "It plays." (See verbs, page 8.)

Prices are rising **nowadays**. (*Not*, **anymore**—see page 78.)

COMPOUND SUBJECTS

Two or more nouns can work together to form a **compound subject**. If the two nouns are joined by "and," both subject and verb are **plural**.

Chi-Chi and Jasmine, former Rockettes, **are** now mud wrestlers.
(compound subject) *(plural verb)*

If compound subjects are joined by "nor" or "or," the verb must agree with the word that follows "nor" or "or." Here's a sentence that uses "neither . . . nor":

 Right
Neither the Rolling Stones **nor** Madonna **lacks** self-esteem.
(singular verb)

 Wrong
Neither the Rolling Stones **nor** Madonna **lack** self-esteem.
(plural verb)

? **Why?** "Madonna," which follows "nor," is singular. Use the singular verb form "lacks." Say, "She lacks."

This example uses "either . . . or."

 Right
Either Robin Hood **or** his men always **bring** home dinner.
(plural verb)

 Wrong
Either Robin Hood **or** his men always **brings** home dinner.
(singular verb)

? **Why?** "Men," which follows "or," is plural. Use the plural verb form "bring." Say, "They bring."

Mimi bought caviar **for her and me.** (*Not,* **for she and I**—see pages 18–19.)

Pronouns

ALVIN AND HOBBES by Bill Watterson

Pronouns are substitutes. Pronouns take the place of nouns.

Samantha called **Big Bird** on her toy phone.
  (noun)   *(noun)*

She called **him** on her toy phone.
(pronoun)   *(pronoun)*

Pro means "for." A pronoun *stands for* a noun.

PRONOUNS AS SUBJECTS OR OBJECTS

Pronouns have different forms, depending on what job the pronoun does in the sentence. Using the wrong pronoun form is a common grammar glitch. To know which form to use, figure out whether the pronoun is the *subject* of a sentence or a clause. Use the *subjective* form if that's the case. (What's a subject? See page 43.)

Chart 1: Subjective Form

Person	Singular	Plural
First Person	I	we
Second Person	you	you
Third Person	he, she, it (who, whoever)	they

David **bragged about** how he slew Goliath. (*Not,* **bragged on**—see page 93.)

17

TIP: With forms of the verb "be," use *subjective* pronouns, such as "This is she" or "It was they." (This rule is bending. While we can't wrap our tongues around "It's me!" or "That's him," we recognize that the use of objective pronouns with "be" verbs is becoming more common.)

Is the pronoun the *object* of a verb or a preposition? If so, use the *objective* form. (What's an object? See page 44.)

Chart 2: Objective Form

Person	Singular	Plural
First Person	me	us
Second Person	you	you
Third Person	him, her, it (whom, whomever)	them

TIP: The pronoun "you" stays the same in both singular and plural forms.

THE FAR SIDE by Gary Larson

"So, then ... Would that be 'us the people' or 'we the people?'"

Things are **looking bad** on the freeway. (*Not,* **looking badly**—see page 79.)

In simple sentences, it's easy to choose the right pronoun. Like nouns, pronouns can be subjects:

Right

We loved Babyface's concert.

Wrong

Us loved Babyface's concert.

? **Why?** You probably wouldn't say, "Us loved . . . ," but do you know why? "We" is the subject of the sentence. Use the *subjective* form of the pronoun—"we," *not* "us." (See chart 1, page 17.)

Like nouns, pronouns can also be **objects of verbs**.

Right

Oprah called **me.**

Wrong

Oprah called **I.**

? **Why?** You probably wouldn't say, ". . . called I." Here's why. "Me" is the object of the verb "called." Use the *objective* form of the pronoun—"me," *not* "I." (See chart 2, page 18)

Pronouns can also be **objects of prepositions**. After a preposition, always use the *objective* form of a pronoun. (See chart 2, page 18.) What's a preposition? See pages 31–33.

Send the plastic roses **to him.**
　　　　　(preposition) (objective pronoun)
Eating fast food is **beneath them.**
　　　　　(preposition) (objective pronoun)

Right	**Wrong**
for her	for she
between you and me	between you and I
to Sue and me	to Sue and I
with Yuko and them	with Yuko and they

The band played **well.** (*Not,* **good**—see page 81.)

PRONOUNS AS POSSESSIVES

Pronouns can also show **possession**.

Chart 3: Possessive Form

Person	Singular	Plural
First Person	**my, mine**	**our, ours**
Second Person	**your, yours**	**your, yours**
Third Person	**his, her, hers, its (whose)**	**their, theirs**

Make the form of the pronoun agree with the noun it stands for.

 Right
The ostrich ruffled **its** feathers.

 Wrong
The ostrich ruffled **their** feathers.

? **Why?** The feathers belong to one ostrich. Use the singular "its," *not* the plural "their."

Don't confuse possessive pronouns with contractions.

 Right
Does **your** computer crash daily, like mine?

 Wrong
Does **you're** computer crash daily, like mine?

? **Why?** "Your" shows possession: your computer. The contraction "you're" stands for "you are."

Beware of easy-to-make mistakes such as these: "The snowmobile lost **it's** traction" or "**Your** so fine."
<small>(it is)   (possessive pronoun)</small>

(See page 59 for more on contractions.)

TIP: Possessive *its* never splits.

Jenny and Kim **have thrown** a great party. (*Not*, **has thrown**—see page 16.)

PRONOUNS IN COMPOUND SUBJECTS

The going gets tougher when pronouns work together with other pronouns or with nouns to form the **compound subject** of a sentence.

Right

Jamie and I patted the baby hippo.
(compound subject)

Wrong

Jamie and me patted the baby hippo.
(compound subject)

? **Why?** "Jamie and I" is the compound subject of the sentence. Use "I," not "me." "I" is *subjective*. "Me" is *objective*. (See chart 1, page 17.)

TIP: Remove the words "Jamie and." You wouldn't say, "Me patted the baby hippo."

It's easy to get only *part* of the compound subject right.

Right

She and he got hitched in Las Vegas.
(compound subject)

Wrong

She and him got hitched in Las Vegas.
(compound subject)

? **Why?** "She and he" is the compound subject of the sentence. Both pronouns should be *subjective*. Use "he," not "him." "She" is *subjective*. "Him" is *objective*. (See chart 1, page 17.)

TIP: Remove the words "She and." You wouldn't say, "Him got married."

Bouquets sell for $4. (*Not*, **Bouquet's**—see page 67.)

PRONOUNS IN COMPOUND OBJECTS

Pronouns can work together with nouns and with other pronouns to form the **compound object** of a verb.

Right

Alice beat **Gus and him** to the finish line.
(compound object)

Wrong

Alice beat **Gus and he** to the finish line.
(compound object)

? **Why?** "Gus and him" is the compound object of the verb "beat." Use "him," not "he." "Him" is *objective.* "He" is *subjective.* (See chart 2, page 18.)

TIP: Take out the words "Gus and." You wouldn't say, "Alice beat he."

PRONOUNS AS OBJECTS OF PREPOSITIONS

Pronouns can also work with nouns and with other pronouns to form the **object** of a preposition. (See pages 31–33 for more about prepositions.)

Right

Between **you and me**, girdles are ridiculous.
(compound object)

Wrong

Between **you and I**, girdles are ridiculous.
(compound object)

? **Why?** "Between" is a preposition. Prepositions take the *objective* form of pronouns. "You and me" is the compound object of "between." (See chart 2, page 18.)

Jodie **has never run** out of ideas. (*Not,* **has never ran**—see page 10.)

PRONOUN-NOUN AGREEMENT

B. C. by Johnny Hart

Note: To these hapless cavemen, the YOU sculpture is a work of art (and singular). Say, "*It* is here." In all other cases, "You is here" would be incorrect.

Pronouns must agree with the nouns they replace in person, number, and gender. Make the pronoun agree with the closest noun *before* it (the *antecedent*).

 Right

The **IRS** audits whenever **it** can.

(singular noun)   *(singular pronoun)*

 Wrong

The **IRS** audits whenever **they** can.

(singular noun)   *(plural pronoun)*

? **Why?** "IRS" (the Internal Revenue Service) is a singular noun. The pronoun that replaces "IRS" must agree in person and number. Use the singular pronoun "it," *not* the plural pronoun "they." Say, "*It* audits." (See chart 1, page 17.)

Don't **try to** compete. (*Not,* **try and** compete—see page 6.)

PRONOUNS THAT END IN "SELF"

HEATHCLIFF by George Gately

"DON'T FORGET YOUR TOWEL."

Pronouns that end with *self* (singular) or *selves* (plural) are called *reflexives*.

Pronouns that end with *self* must refer to a person or thing in the same clause or sentence:

I polished the Porsche **myself**.

Pronouns That End In "Self"

Person	Singular	Plural
First Person	**myself**	**ourselves**
Second Person	**yourself**	**yourselves**
Third Person	**himself, herself, itself** (*never* hisself)	**themselves** (*never* theirselves)

 Right
Captain Garcia and **I** welcome you aboard.

 Wrong
Captain Garcia and **myself** welcome you aboard.

? **Why?** "Myself" does not refer to anyone in the sentence.

Pronouns that end with *self* help emphasize a person or the people to which they refer. Correct uses of pronouns that end with *self*:

▶ Referring to the subject of a clause or sentence.

You fix the faucet **yourself**!

▶ Emphasizing a person or thing.

Jacqueline herself built the log cabin.

Don't substitute reflexive pronouns for objective pronouns:

"Hand your ticket to **me**," *not* "Hand your ticket to **myself**."

Marie's brains and talent **guarantee** her success. (*Not*, **guarantees**—see page 16.)

INDEFINITE PRONOUNS

Some pronouns are **indefinite**. They refer to persons, places, or things in general. Indefinite pronouns can be singular or plural. Verbs that follow indefinite pronouns have to agree in person and number. (See page 11 for more on verb agreement.)

Singular: anybody, anyone, each, either, every, everybody, everyone, neither, nobody, no one, nothing, one

Plural: both, few, many, several

Using a singular indefinite pronoun:

 Right
Nobody knows why Bubbles dumped Bronco.
(indefinite pronoun) (singular verb)

 Wrong
Nobody know why Bubbles dumped Bronco.
(indefinite pronoun) (plural verb)

? **Why?** "Nobody" is a singular indefinite pronoun. Use a singular verb. (See page 11.)

Using a plural indefinite pronoun:

 Right
Yo-Yo Ma plays cello. Billy Joel plays piano.
Both are musicians. *Or*, **both** of them **are** musicians.
(indefinite pronoun) (plural verb)

 Wrong
Yo-Yo Ma plays cello. Billy Joel plays piano.
Both is musicians. *Or*, **both** of them **is** musicians.
(indefinite pronoun) (singular verb)

? **Why?** "Both" is a plural indefinite pronoun. Use a plural verb. Say, "*They* are." (See page 11.)

He has only **himself** to blame. (*Not*, **hisself**—see page 24.)

25

But watch out! Some indefinite pronouns can be **singular** *or* **plural**. (See page 14.) Should you use a singular or a plural verb? Look at the key word(s) following the pronoun.

Singular *or* **Plural**: all, any, most, none, some

TIP: Memorize these five pronouns—*all, any, most, none, some*. They change like chameleons, matching what follows them.

Examples:

> In our house, **most** of the fudge cake **disappears**.
>   *(indefinite pronoun)*   *(singular verb)*
> ("Cake" disappears. Say, "It disappears.")

> In our house, **most** of the pretzels **disappear**.
>   *(indefinite pronoun)*   *(plural verb)*
> ("Pretzels" disappear. Say, "They disappear.")

> **All** of the student housing **is rented**.
> *(indefinite pronoun)*   *(singular verb)*
> ("Housing" is rented. Say, "It is rented.")

> **All** of the students **eat** pasta on Mondays.
> *(indefinite pronoun)*   *(plural verb)*
> ("Students" eat. Say, "They eat.")

> **None** of the resort **was** damaged by the tornado.
> *(indefinite pronoun)*   *(singular verb)*
> ("Resort" was. Say, "It was.")

> **None** of the resorts **were** damaged by the tornado.
> *(indefinite pronoun)*   *(plural verb)*
> ("Resorts" were. Say, "They were.")

Bette takes golf **seriously**. (*Not*, **serious**—see page 36.)

WHO OR WHOM?

BEETLE BAILEY by Mort Walker

Who—Always a Subject

The pronoun **who** is always the subject of a sentence or clause. (See page 43 to learn about subjects.) **Who** is never an object.

Right

Who ordered the anchovies?
(subject)

Wrong

Whom ordered the anchovies?

?

Why? "Who" is the *subject* of the sentence. It stands for the person who ordered the anchovies. Use the *subjective* pronoun— "who," *not* "whom." (See chart 1, page 17.)

Who runs this office?

I wonder **who** baked snickerdoodles?

Is Nicky the one **who** scored the goal?

Note: In casual writing and speech, "who" is more commonly used, except following prepositions, when "whom" is still generally favored (see page 28). For formal writing and speech, however, it's wise to stick with the rules on this page and the next.

Waltzing is **different from** line dancing. (*Not,* **different than**—see page 80.)

Whom—Always an Object

The pronoun **whom** is never a subject of a sentence or clause. Use **whom** as the object of a verb or of a preposition.

Whom as the Object of a Verb

 Right
Duke called **whom**?
<small>*(object)*</small>

 Wrong
Duke called **who**?

? **Why?** "Duke" is the subject of the sentence. "Whom" is the *object* of the verb "called." Use the *objective* pronoun—"whom," not "who." (See chart 2, page 18.)

Aunt Olive told **whom** about the affair?

Wendy met **whom** on her trip?

Whom as the Object of a Preposition

Prepositions always take the *objective* form of the pronoun. (See page 19 f more on objects of prepositions.)

 Right
To whom shall I send the million dollars?
(preposition) (object)

 Wrong
To who shall I send the million dollars?

? **Why?** "Whom" is the *object* of the preposition "to." Use the *objective* form of the pronoun—"whom." (See chart 2, page 18.)

Sue watched birds with **whom**?

Meredith's contract was signed by **whom**?

For more hints on "who" and "whom," see page 30.

Pierre **felt bad** about the broken platter. (*Not,* **felt badly**—see pages 79–80.)

THAT OR WHICH?

Both the pronouns **that** and **which** refer to people, animals, or things (objects, ideas, events). Use the pronoun **that** for clauses important (*essential*) to the meaning of the sentence. No commas are needed with "that" clauses.

Right
"The day **that I met Buffy** changed my life," said Luke.
               (essential clause)

Wrong
The day, **that I met Buffy**, changed my life," said Luke.

? **Why?** This isn't an ordinary day. It's the day Luke met Buffy! The words "that I met Buffy" are important (*essential*) to the meaning of the sentence. Use no commas.

Use the pronoun **which** in less important (*nonessential*) clauses. Enclose "which" clauses in commas.

Right
The magazine *George*, **which spoofs politics**, is widely read.
               (nonessential clause)

Wrong
The magazine *George* **which spoofs politics** is widely read.

? **Why?** The words "which spoofs politics" are less important (*nonessential*) to the meaning of the sentence. Set off the "which" clause with commas. (See page 52.)

Note: "That" is a *demonstrative* pronoun—it points out or demonstrates: "that field," "that wolverine." "Which" is an *interrogative* pronoun—it asks or interrogates: "which comb?" "which alley?" (See pages 93–94 for more on pronouns.)

He and his wife have a cool house. (*Not,* **Him and his wife**—see page 21.)

CHOOSING PRONOUNS: SUBJECT-OBJECT HINTS

Sometimes it's hard to know which pronouns to use. Here are some tips for choosing the right pronouns:

▸ **Rearrange the sentence to decide which pronoun to use.**

Who/whom did you need?

Rearranged:
You did need **whom**?
(*subject*)   (*direct object*)

▸ **Add the implied word.**

Mario Andretti scored higher on his driver's test than **I/me**.

"Did" is implied at the end of the sentence.

Andretti scored higher than **I [did score]**.

Use the subjective form, "I," as the subject of the implied clause that starts with "than I [did]." (The conjunction "than" signals an upcoming clause.)

Using "I" or "me" makes a big difference in meaning:

Fred gave Sally more licorice than **I [gave Sally]**.

Fred gave Sally more licorice than **[Fred gave] me**.

▸ **Omit words to help you choose which pronoun to use.**

The joke circulated among **we/us** sailors.

Omit the word "sailors." "Among" is a preposition. Use the objective pronoun—"among *us*." (See page 19 for more on pronouns as objects.)

We/us politicians know that kissing babies counts.

Omit "politicians." "We" is the subject of the sentence. Use the subjective pronoun—"*We* know . . . " (See page 17 for more on pronouns as subjects.)

Today, "A" students **can hardly** get into Harvard. (*Not,* **can't hardly**—see page 37

Prepositions

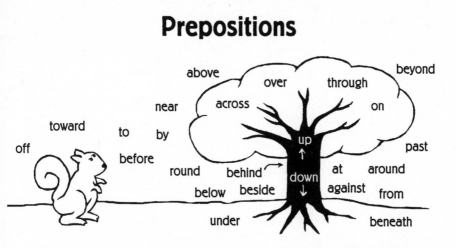

Use the "squirrel and tree" trick to help you remember most prepositions. The squirrel can go **near** the tree, **by** the tree, **up** the tree, **across** the branches, **through** the leaves, **over** the roots, **around** the trunk, **above** the limbs . . .

The skunk sneaked **under** the deck.

The cummerbund barely stretched **around** Pavarotti's middle.

Throughout the palace, the mice were silent.

Prepositions—often small words—show relationships. They can show **position** or **time**. Prepositions can also **compare** or **connect**. (See complete list of prepositions on page 93.)

Prepositions can show **position**—where something happens.

TIP: The word **position** is hidden in the word **preposition.**

Position Prepositions

about	beneath	into	through
above	beside	near	throughout
across	between	off	to
against	beyond	on	toward
along	by	onto	under
around	down	out	underneath
at	from	outside	up
behind	in	over	upon
below	inside	past	within

Who is **supposed** to order the limo? (*Not*, **suppose to**—see page 9.)

Prepositions can show **time**.

Sally always eats pickled herring **before** breakfast.

"I won't walk the plank **until** midnight," said Boris.

Time prepositions:

about   after   before   during   since   until

Prepositions can **compare**.

On Halloween, Kirsten dressed **as** a piano.

Mrs. Skiffle looks just **like** her basset hound.

Comparison prepositions:

as   between   like   unlike

(For more on "as" and "like," see page 42.)

Prepositions can **connect** one group of words with another.

"Cook anything **except** Brussels sprouts or turnips," ordered Sir Markworth.

The men from Mars danced **with** the women from Venus.

Connector prepositions:

about   except   for   from   of   to   with

PREPOSITIONAL PHRASES

Combine a preposition with a noun or pronoun. Presto—you have a **prepositional phrase**. The noun or pronoun becomes the object of the preposition. Prepositions take the *objective* form of a pronoun. (See chart 2, page 18.)

from **them**   to **us**   for Robin and **me**   by **him**

If Nina **were** here, we'd have tea. (*Not,* **was**—see page 94.)

Preposition with a noun	**Preposition** with a pronoun
into the dugout *(preposition)* *(noun)*	into it *(preposition) (pronoun)*
through the doors *(preposition)* *(noun)*	through them *(preposition) (pronoun)*
to Batman *(preposition)* *(noun)*	to him *(preposition) (pronoun)*

·INGLE SLICES by Peter Kohlsaat

I do like it... I really do... but you just can't end your sentences with prepositions...

© 1991, Los Angeles Times Syndicate

Bob's poems to Sheila lose a little of their romance.

"Don't end a sentence with a preposition" used to be a hard and fast rule. In formal writing and speech, avoid ending sentences with prepositions. Use common sense in informal writing and speech.

"Which pan shall I cook the soup **in**?" sounds less stuffy than "**In** which pan shall I cook the soup?"

Likewise, phrases such as, "Where's he **from**?" "Is the doctor **in**?" "Who is that song **by**?" are fine in casual speech.

One exception: don't say, "Where's it **at**?" The preposition "at" that ends this sentence is extra—it's not needed. Just say, "Where is it?"

I **would have** followed you anywhere! (*Not*, **would of**—see page 74.)

Adjectives

9 CHICKWEED LANE by Brooke McEldowney

Adjectives describe (*modify*) nouns. Adjectives add information about a word or phrase.

The president arrived in a **black car** with **gold wheels**.
$\quad\quad\quad\quad\quad\quad\quad$ (*adjective*) (*noun*) $\quad$ (*adjective*) (*noun*)

Roxie wore **false eyelashes** and a **feather boa**.
$\quad\quad\quad$ (*adjective*) (*noun*) $\quad\quad\quad\quad\quad$ (*adjective*) (*noun*)

Several adjectives can describe the same noun. A comma separates adjectives of equal weight. Do not use a comma to separate an adjective from the word it modifies: "small, brown bear." (See page 52 for information on serial commas.)

 Right

Eve adores her **faithful, battered, orange** van.

 Wrong

Eve adores her **faithful, battered orange** van.

 Why? Use a comma if the word "and" would fit between the adjectives and make sense. The van is "faithful" *and* "battered" *and* "orange."

Mary ate **an apple** and a pear. (*Not,* **a apple**—see page 87.)

COMPOUND ADJECTIVES

Compound Adjectives Before Nouns

Compound adjectives consist of two or more words that work together to describe a noun. Together, they express a single thought. Use a hyphen for compound adjectives when they appear before the noun. (See page 62 for more on hyphens.)

Right
Richard devoured five **raspberry-filled** truffles.

Wrong
Richard devoured five **raspberry filled** truffles.

? **Why?** The words "raspberry" and "filled" work together and appear *before* the noun "truffles." Use a hyphen between them.

Compound Adjectives After Nouns

If a compound adjective appears *after* the noun, don't use a hyphen. (See page 62.)

Right
Ms. Gaston's speech was **well polished**.

Wrong
Ms. Gaston's speech was **well-polished**.

? **Why?** The compound adjective "well polished" *follows* the noun "speech." Don't use a hyphen.

Adverb-Adjective Combinations

Watch out for words ending in *ly*—they are often adverbs. Do not use hyphens between adverb-adjective combinations.

Felix's **neatly organized** desk only confused Oscar.
   (adverb)   *(adjective)*

"Neatly" is an adverb that tells *how* Felix's desk is organized. Use no hyphen with adverb-adjective combos, whether they fall before or after the noun they modify.

You **should have gone**. (*Not,* **should have went**—see page 10.)

Adverbs

Adverbs describe (*modify*) verbs, adjectives, or other adverbs. They often tell *how, when, where, how much,* or *to what extent.* Here are some examples:

How?	When?	Where?
sweetly	tomorrow	there
fiercely	tonight	here
well	soon	everywhere
simply	now	nowhere

When Felicity sang, Howard laughed **rudely**.
(verb) *(adverb)*

How did Howard laugh? **Rudely.**

As the chart above shows, not all adverbs end in **ly**.

▸ Hayley's babysitter arrives **soon**.
(verb) *(adverb)*

   When will the babysitter arrive? **Soon.**

▸ Rob's band played **well**.
(verb) *(adverb)*

   How did Rob's band play? **Well.**

Adverbs can modify adjectives.

▸ Savvy politicians are **never** shy.
(adverb) *(adjective)*

   When are savvy politicians shy? **Never.** The adverb "never" modifies the adjective "shy."

Adverbs can modify adverbs.

▸ The vulture flew **frighteningly close**.
(verb) *(adverb)* *(adverb)*

   Where did the vulture fly? **Close.** *How* close?
Frighteningly close.

(Note: Some words can be either adjectives or adverbs—for instance, *fast, slow, good, bad, well.*)

Nate invited **Erin and me** for dinner. (*Not,* **Erin and I**—see page 19.)

DOUBLE NEGATIVES

Some words are negative—they give a sense of "not" or "no" in a sentence. Common negative words are *no, not, none, never, nothing, hardly, barely, scarcely.* Avoid double negatives—using two negatives to say "no."

Right
There was **hardly** time to grab a taxi**.**

Wrong
There was**n't hardly** time to grab a taxi.

Why? "Wasn't" is short for "was *not.*" "Hardly" and the "not" in "wasn't" are both negatives. Together, they form a double negative. Use one word or the other, but not both.

TIP: Contractions ending in **n't** are negative. They connect verbs with "not." Apostrophes take the place of missing letters. Do not link negative contractions with other negatives.

Verb + Not	Contraction	Verb + Not	Contraction
do not	don't	have not	haven't
did not	didn't	had not	hadn't
will not	won't	cannot	can't
would not	wouldn't	should not	shouldn't

Right
Mr. Snipple does**n't** know anything.
Or, Mr. Snipple knows **nothing.**

Wrong
Mr. Snipple does**n't** know **nothing.**

Why? "Doesn't" is short for "does *not.*" The "not" in "doesn't" and the negative word "nothing" form a double negative. Use one word or the other, but not both.

I have **fewer** quarters than you do. (*Not,* **less**—see page 81.)

COMPARISONS

Adjectives and some adverbs can be used to compare things. The *comparative* degree (**er** or **more**) compares two things. The *superlative* degree (**est** or **most**) compares three or more things. With most one-syllable words and some two-syllable words, add **er** for the comparative and **est** for the superlative.

Positive	Comparative *(compares two things)*	Superlative *(compares more than two things)*
crisp	crisper	crispest
fast	faster	fastest
mild	milder	mildest
sleepy	sleepier	sleepiest
sturdy	sturdier	sturdiest

TIP: If a word ends in **y**, change the **y** to **i**, then add **er** or **est**.

With some two-syllable words and with words that have three or more syllables, add **more** for the comparative and **most** for the superlative.

Positive	Comparative *(compares two things)*	Superlative *(compares more than two things)*
modern	more modern	most modern
slowly	more slowly	most slowly
fortunate	more fortunate	most fortunate
enthusiastic	more enthusiastic	most enthusiastic

Use **less** or **least** to show lesser degrees of comparison: *less modern, less enthusiastic, least fortunate.*

TIP: Most dictionaries will show you which forms of a word to use for comparison.

A few comparisons are irregular: *good, better, best; bad, worse, worst.*

Ron felt **as if** he should save his cat Prissy. (*Not,* **like**—see page 42.)

DOUBLE COMPARISONS

Don't use **double comparisons**, such as *more sturdier, most mildest, more worse, most boldest,* or *more better.* Use one form or the other, not both.

 Right
Pineapples are **sweeter** than grapefruit.

 Wrong
Pineapples are **more sweeter** than grapefruit.

? **Why?** "Sweeter" already compares the two fruits. Don't use both "more" and "sweeter." That's a double comparison.

 Right
Mrs. Rockefeller is the **richest** woman I know.

Wrong
Mrs. Rockefeller is the **most richest** woman I know.

? **Why?** "Richest" is already as rich as Mrs. Rockefeller can get. Don't use both "most" and "richest." That's a double comparison.

TIP: Another double comparison is "most unique." The adjective "unique" means "without equal, one of a kind." Say, "That violin is unique," *not* "That violin is the most unique." The same applies to the adjective "perfect."

Know the Numbers—Two or More Than Two?

 Right
Margot was the **quickest** of the three girls.

Wrong
Margot was the **quicker** of the three girls.

? **Why?** "Quicker" compares two things. "Quickest" compares more than two.

Who's on first? (*Not,* **Whose**—see pages 20 and 59.)

Interjections

BABY BLUES by Rick Kirkman and Jerry Scott

Interjections are outsiders. They express feelings but aren't officially part of a sentence. Here are some examples:

ah	good night, nurse	ouch
ah-ha	hey	ugh
alas	hooray	well
all right	no	whew
dear me	no way	wow

Marks of punctuation usually follow interjections. Use a comma after mild interjections (well, goodness). For strong interjections (eeek! rats!), use an exclamation point and capitalize the next word, unless the interjection is part of a quotation:

Mild:
Alas, James Beard's angel food cake flopped.

Strong:
Hey! Those are *my* running shorts!

Interjection in a quotation:
"**Good grief!**" said Charlie Brown.

Save interjections for informal or personal writing. You may see interjections in advertising, but avoid them in formal writing.

Andrea **saw** kangaroos in Australia. (*Not,* **seen**—see page 96.)

Conjunctions

Conjunctions connect groups of words or parts of a sentence. Here are some conjunctions:

and	but	since	though
as	if	so	unless
because	or	than	while

Bessie **and** Daisy mooed happily.
(conjunction)

Since it's St. Patrick's Day, I'm wearing green underwear.
(conjunction)

You're a better swimmer **than I.** [Implied: **than I am.**]
(conjunction)

Julie couldn't reach Randy **because** he'd gone surfing.
(conjunction)

But is it okay to start a sentence with a conjunction? It's fine—just don't do it too often. *And* avoid it in formal writing.

Some conjunctions work in pairs:

both/and	neither/nor	whether/or not
either/or	not only/but also	

Neither Romeo **nor** Juliet knew the whole truth.
(conjunction)   *(conjunction)*

She **not only** runs *Latina* **but also** writes articles for it.
(conjunction)   *(conjunction)*

Jana's **too** smart for that job. (*Not, to*—see page 91.)

41

As and Like

Baffled by "as" and "like"? Both can compare. When linked with other words, they form *similes*, which compare two dissimilar things.

bright as a comet   eats like a horse

"As" can be both a conjunction and a preposition.

As—*when used as a conjunction:*
"As" is a conjunction when followed by a verb.

As Rome **burned**, Nero fiddled.
(conjunction)   *(verb)*

"As" often teams with "if" or "though" to form the conjunctions "as if" or "as though."

She felt **as if** she'd been tricked.

He felt **as though** she hadn't.

As—*when used as a preposition:*
"As" is a preposition when followed by a comparison and no verb.

As an animal lover, I hate fox hunting.
(preposition)

Like—*the preposition:*
"Like" is a preposition, not a conjunction.

Like his brother Don, Dave loves jazz.
(preposition)

 Right
Like the "church lady," Delphine wore a helmet hairdo.
(preposition)

Wrong
Like I said, Delphine wore a helmet hairdo.
(preposition)

? **Why?** In the right example, "church lady" is the object of the preposition "like." Together, the words compare. In the wrong example, the verb "said" follows "like." There, "like" is incorrectly used as if it were a conjunction. (See page 41 to learn about conjunctions.)

Is William a "techno-Luddite"? (*Not*, "techno-Luddite?"—see page 58.)

PART II:
BUILDING BLOCKS

THE SENTENCE

A **sentence** expresses a complete thought. Verbs, nouns, and other words work together to form meaning in sentences. Sentences have two parts—the subject and the predicate.

THE SUBJECT

The **subject** tells *who* or *what* the sentence is about.

The **joke** flopped.
(subject)

A **complete subject** includes the subject and all the words that describe it.

Herbie's gourmet food astonished the fishermen.
(complete subject)

In sentences that command or order, "you" is an implied subject.

Stop that! [Implied: You stop that!]

Answer the phone. [Implied: You answer the phone.]

CHICKWEED LANE by Brooke McEldowney

Dieter **doesn't live** here anymore. (*Not*, **don't live**—see page 11.)

THE PREDICATE

The **predicate** tells what is happening to the subject. The predicate includes the verb and all the words related to the verb.

Eighty wedding guests ate nine submarine sandwiches.

    (complete subject)   *(predicate)*

The **direct object** of the verb tells *who* or *what* receives the action of the verb.

Karen met **Jon** at Club Med. [Karen met *whom?* Jon.]
    (verb) *(direct object)*

Greg caught **a huge marlin**. [Greg caught *what?* A marlin.]
    (verb)   *(direct object)*

DIAGRAMMING

Different parts of speech fit together like pieces of a puzzle. When linked, they build sentences.

MOTHER GOOSE & GRIMM by Mike Peters

Diagramming sentences shows how the parts connect to express ideas. The main subject and predicate appear on a single line. Other words branch off, adding details to the sentence.

▸ Jerry ran.

subject	*predicate*
Jerry	**ran**
(noun)	*(verb)*

I'm going to lie out in the sun. (*Not*, **lay**—see pages 83–84.)

▸ Mr. O'Hara loved Irish stew.

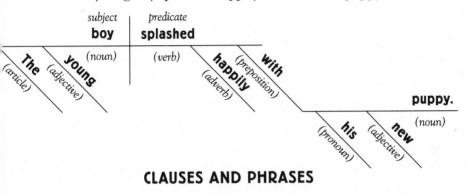

▸ The young boy splashed happily with his new puppy.

CLAUSES AND PHRASES

Clauses

A **clause** is a group of related words that has both a subject and a predicate. A clause can be a complete sentence or a part of a sentence.

An independent clause forms a complete thought. Independent clauses can stand alone as simple sentences.

Tess called Frederick a nincompoop.
(noun) (verb)
(independent clause—simple sentence)

A dependent clause depends on the rest of the sentence to make sense. Dependent clauses cannot stand alone, even if they have a subject and a predicate. They do not form complete sentences.

Although the Bulldogs tried, they lost the game.
(dependent clause—not a simple sentence)

Norman visits Fiji twice a year **because he loves it.**
(dependent clause—not a simple sentence)

Melissa ran **farther** than Charlie. (*Not,* **further**—see page 81.)

45

A comma sometimes separates one clause from another.

While she waited at the light, Bipsy did her nails.
       (*dependent clause*)   (*independent clause*)

The dependent clauses "although the Bulldogs tried," "because he loves it," and "while she waited at the light" cannot stand alone. They depend on the rest of the sentence for meaning. (See page 29 for more information on essential and nonessential clauses.)

Phrases

A **phrase** is a group of related words without a subject and predicate combination. A phrase is never a complete sentence.

saved by the bell   in the morning
a young stranger   practicing his juggling skills
building a portfolio

As with clauses, punctuation with phrases depends on the job they do in the sentence. In the sentence below, the phrase "Guarding Abe Lincoln" acts as the subject of the sentence and needs no comma. Without this phrase, the sentence doesn't make sense:

Guarding Abe Lincoln was an honor for Allan Pinkerton.
   (*phrase*)

Use commas to set off phrases not important to the meaning of a sentence. These sentences make sense without the phrases that are set off by commas:

Don hates broccoli, **especially for dessert.**
               (*phrase*)

Wiping her brow, Jessica sighed.
  (*phrase*)

Mr. Hotchkiss, **the new bandleader,** wore a striped bow tie.
           (*phrase*)

Clauses and phrases can work together to form sentences.

Against Ludwig's better judgment, he called Sara.
      (*phrase*)   (*clause*)

Carolyn and Len outdid **themselves.** (*Not,* **theirselves**—see page 24.)

46

PRONOUN REFERENCE PROBLEMS

Unclear pronoun reference can cause problems. Be clear about which noun a pronoun refers to. Make the pronoun agree with the closest noun *before* it. (That noun is called the *antecedent*. "Ante" means before.)

After Todd told **Larry, he** told the world.

Who is the gossip? Todd or Larry? "He" is closest to the noun "Larry." If Todd is the gossip, change the sentence to

After Todd told Larry, **Todd** told the world.

MISPLACED MODIFIERS

A **modifier** is a word or group of words that describes another.

Modifiers can be adjectives:

Lee made a **brilliant** statement.
             (*adjective*)   (*noun*)

Modifiers can be adverbs:

Betty bowled **beautifully**.
   (*verb*)   (*adverb*)

Modifiers can be clauses or phrases:

The man **who ducked out the back door** was my date.
  (*noun*)   (*clause modifies noun*)

The girl **with green hair** did a fan dance.
 (*noun*) (*phrase modifies noun*)

Funny things happen when modifiers appear too far away from the words they modify.

- Robin soaked the foot **he sprained in ice water**.
  An odd injury—Robin sprained his foot in ice water?

- John hit a triple to left field, **which flew over the fence**.
  Left field flew over the fence?

Kirsten designed the **company's** logo. (*Not*, **companys'** logo—see page 61.)

Three Tips for Avoiding Misplaced Modifiers:

Keep modifiers close to the words modified.
Keep subject and verb together.
Be clear about which noun a pronoun stands for.

DANGLING PARTICIPIAL PHRASES

Another type of misplaced modifier is the dangling participial phrase. **Participles** are verb forms ending with *ing* in the present tense and *d* or *ed* in the past. A few past participles end in *t* or have irregular forms. (See pages 95–96 for a list of irregular verb forms.)

> dribbling   skating   scaled   burned *or* burnt

Combine a participle with other words to create a **participial phrase.** Participial phrases act as adjectives.

> filled with hope   cleaning the bathroom   jumping overboard

Keep participial phrases close to the words they modify. Otherwise the phrase dangles and gets confusing.

> ▸ **When swimming across the lake, the boat** always followed Judith.
>
> Whoops! Looks like the boat is swimming, not Judith.
>
> *Better:*
>
> When Judith swam across the lake, the boat always followed.

> ▸ **Loaded with bonbons, the waiter** carried the tray.
>
> The tray is loaded with bonbons, not the waiter (unless she's been snacking heavily!).
>
> *Better:*
>
> The waiter carried the tray that was loaded with bonbons.

Congress and the president **are** gridlocked. (*Not,* **is**—see page 16.)

▸ **A red car** was reported **stolen by the Spooner Police**.

> The police didn't steal the car; they reported it as stolen.
>
> *Better:*
>
> The Spooner Police reported that a red car was stolen.
>
> ("Stolen" is the past participle of the irregular verb "steal.")

KINDS OF SENTENCES

Verbs, nouns, and other types of words work together to form sentences. There are four kinds of sentences—*declarative, interrogative, imperative,* and *exclamatory*.

Declarative: States a fact, gives information. Declarative sentences have a subject and a verb and sometimes a direct object.

> Hilary grows glorious roses.
> When I was young, I roller-skated.
> Jerry plays the viola.

Interrogative: Asks a question. Interrogative sentences often start with words that ask questions, such as *who, why, what, where, which, when, how*.

> Carol, are you out of chocolate?
> What time will Joanne's plane arrive?
> How is Aisha doing?

Imperative: Gives an order. The subject "you" is often implied. The sentence may be just one or two words long.

> Run! [Implied: You run!]
> Eat your spinach! [Implied: You eat your spinach!]
> Angus, do something about those ants!

Exclamatory: Expresses strong emotion.

> You're fired!
> I quit!
> We will not stand for this nonsense!

Ashley was quicker **than he**. (*Not,* **than him**—see page 41.)

PART III:
PUNCTUATION POINTERS

PUNCTUATION AS TRAFFIC SIGNALS

Punctuation is a code to help readers ride smoothly through writing. Think of punctuation marks as traffic signals:

.   **Period = Stop Sign**
Come to a full stop. Then go on—no sliding through.

,   **Comma = Flashing Yellow Light**
Slow down, look left and right, then continue.

;   **Semicolon = Flashing Red Light**
Stop briefly; forge ahead.

:   **Colon = Arrow or Road Sign**
Listen up! What follows explains or adds information.

( ) and —   **Parentheses and Dashes = Detour**
Take a quick detour—then proceed.

Other Punctuation

" "   **Quotation Marks**

'   **Apostrophes**

-      **Hyphens**

?   **Question Marks**

!   **Exclamation Points**

(For ellipses . . . , see appendix, page 89.)

I'd go if the concert **were** free. (*Not,* **was**—see page 94.)

PERIODS

Periods (.) are stop signs. Put one space after a period ending a sentence. Use periods:

▸ At the end of sentences that state a fact (*declarative sentences*) or give an order (*imperative sentences*). (See page 49.)

> Blanche loves surfing the Internet. (This states a fact.)
>
> Barkley, fetch me my slippers. (This gives an order.)

▸ After numbers in a list.

Short list for Speaker of the House:
1. George of the Jungle
2. Minnie Mouse
3. Kermit the Frog

▸ With many abbreviations.

Dr. Clamper
Ms. Lu
The Rev. Jesse Jackson
I love gooey desserts, e.g., sundaes, custards, and eclairs.

Remember—no sliding through stop signs! Using a comma instead of a period creates a run-on sentence.

Right
The Arizona Wildcats won. The Kentucky Wildcats lost.

Wrong
The Arizona Wildcats won, the Kentucky Wildcats lost.

? **Why?** These are two complete thoughts. End both sentences with a period. You could also link them with a semicolon or a conjunction. (See pages 41 and 53.)

> Marla and Bev work by day; they write by night.
>   *not*
> Marla and Bev work by day, they write by night.

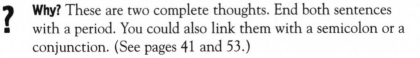

Lie down, Bingo! (*Not*, **Lay** —see pages 83–84.)

COMMAS

B. C. by Johnny Hart

Commas (**,**) signal a pause in the action, like a flashing yellow light. Put one space after a comma. Use commas:

▶ After a long introductory phrase or clause.

> While heating last week's leftovers, Susie Jo read *The Star*.

▶ To separate elements in a list or series (called *serial commas*). Commas help make ideas clear.

> Erika says a good gym has music, equipment, and cute guys.

Unclear:
> Jim shopped in the children's maternity and toy departments.

Clear:
> Jim shopped in the children's, maternity, and toy departments.

▶ To separate clauses joined by conjunctions, such as *and, but, for, or, nor,* or *so*.

> Julia loved Justin, **but** he seemed oblivious.

▶ To set off a phrase that describes a noun or phrase.

> **David Copperfield, the magician,** has vanished.
>   *(noun)*   *(phrase describes noun)*

> Pat's **ancient tent, a green canvas monster,** collapsed last night.
>   *(phrase)*   *(phrase describes phrase)*

▶ To set off a less important clause. Use commas with "which" clauses. (See page 29.)

> Wigs, which come in all colors, are great for bad hair days.

There was no lobster on Carole's plate. (*Not,* **Their**—see page 85.)

▸ In direct address or for greetings in friendly letters.

Henry, shape up.   I'm speaking to you, Judy.

Dear Joel,   My dearest Buttercup,

▸ To separate names and titles; to separate names of cities, states, and countries.

Jasper Sludge, president of Sludge Sanitation, hates recycling.

Siren, Wisconsin
  (city, state)
Guadalajara, Jalisco, Mexico
  (city, state, country)
Paris, France
  (city, country)

SEMICOLONS

In sentences, semicolons (;) are flashing red lights. They make readers apply the brakes before going on. Put one space after a semi-colon. Use semicolons:

▸ To link two closely related thoughts.

Of course my stomach's rumbling; it's lunchtime.

▸ To separate two main clauses.

Many criminals leave clues; detectives follow the trail.

(You could also turn these two thoughts into separate sentences, or link them with a conjunction.)

▸ To separate a list of items that already includes commas, such as names and titles or cities and states.

The Century Club's new officers are Rose Harper, president; Hans Klaus, vice president; Leticia Perkins, treasurer.

Buy our Wild Vacation Package for Sleepy Eye, Minnesota; Slippery Rock, Pennsylvania; and Snowflake, Arizona!

After dinner, **we** men did the dishes. (*Not*, **us**—see page 17.)

▸ To separate a sentence that is long and complex.

> Stewart moved his mother to a new apartment in Naples; this forced a winnowing of her belongings of fifty years, including all clothing, papers, and knickknacks.

COLONS

Colons (:) are arrows or road signs. They are more formal, signaling that a list, explanation, or long quotation follows. Put one space after a colon. Use colons:

▸ To introduce a list.

> Percival's luncheon menu includes these items: caviar, biscuits, anchovies, and spinach quiche.

(Note: No capital on "caviar.")

▸ With a greeting in a business letter.

> Dear Ms. Pocketwrench:

▸ Before an explanation, even if it forms a short sentence.

> Understanding the opposite sex is impossible: Men and women think differently.

▸ With direct quotations or if a complete sentence follows the colon. These are the only times you use a capital letter after the colon.

> When it comes to the stock market, I stick to this maxim: "Fools rush in where angels fear to tread."

(Capital letter on "Fools"—it begins a quotation.)

Our course is clear: Proceed first to the chocolate box.

(Capital letter on "Proceed"—it begins a complete sentence.)

> Tournament organizers were frustrated: The caddies were on strike, and weather threatened the opening ceremonies.

(Capital letter on "The"—it begins a complete sentence.)

What **effect** does jazz have on me? (*Not*, **affect**—see page 78.)

PARENTHESES AND DASHES

Parentheses ( ) and dashes — mark detours that interrupt the reader. They add extra information or show a break in thought. Put no spaces before or after a dash.

▸ Parentheses (more formal) enclose material that adds less essential information. The sentence would still make sense if you vacuumed out the words inside the parentheses. Put a space before opening parentheses and after closing parentheses.

> Take your camping supplies (tent, flashlight, canteen, and hiking boots) to the parking lot.

> The Clown College graduates (Tilly, Stringbean, Jig-Jiggity, and Squirt) rode tricycles across the stage to get their diplomas.

In both examples, using commas instead of parentheses would confuse the reader.

▸ Dashes—more informal—draw attention or add information. Dashes help emphasize words, phrases, or clauses.

> Television—though I never watch it myself—has become the national obsession.

> In my opinion, Jackson—a serious flirt—is not husband material.

In both examples, commas would also be correct.

With a typewriter, make a dash with two hyphens: --

For information on em dashes (—) and en dashes (–), see appendix, pages 88–89.

José **saw** the Golden Gate Bridge. (*Not,* **seen**—see page 96.)

QUOTATION MARKS

Use quotation marks (**" "**):

▸ To quote someone's exact words.

"You must do the thing you think you cannot do," said Eleanor Roosevelt.

▸ To enclose the titles of poems, songs, stories, book chapters, individual episodes of radio or TV shows, and articles. (Longer works usually are set in italics. See page 92.)

Poem: "Dreams" by Langston Hughes

Story: "The Tortoise and the Hare" by Aesop

Song: "The Way You Look Tonight" by Dorothy Fields and Jerome Kern

Article: "Dow Hits 10,000" by Alan Greenspan

▸ To set off individual words.

Track star Wilma Rudolph's nickname was "Skeeter."

Rules of the road can help you when punctuating with quotation marks. Learn these "inside-outside" rules.

Periods (**.**) and commas (**,**) = always **inside** quotation marks

---

 Right
Robert Frost wrote the poem "The Road Not Taken."

 Wrong
Robert Frost wrote the poem "The Road Not Taken**"**.

 Why? Periods and commas always go *inside* quotation marks.

Lay your cards on the table. (*Not,* **Lie**—see pages 83–84.)

Colons (:) and semicolons (;) = always **outside** quotation marks

 Right
He's no "spring chicken"; he's an old buzzard.

 Wrong
He's no "spring chicken;" he's an old buzzard.

? **Why?** Colons and semicolons always go *outside* quotation marks.

Question marks (?), exclamation points (!), and dashes (—)
= **inside** *or* **outside**

These three marks (?, !, and —) go inside *or* outside depending on their use. They go *inside* the quotation marks when they apply only to what is quoted.

"...?"   "...!"   "...—"

Question mark inside a quotation:

 Right
Maurice snapped, "What's the bottom line?"

 Wrong
Maurice snapped, "What's the bottom line"?

? **Why?** Only Maurice's words are a question, not the whole sentence. Place the question mark *inside* the end quotation mark.

Exclamation point inside a quotation:

The airplane banner read: "JANELLE—MARRY ME!"

Dash inside a quotation:

"I'll get the groc—" Wayne froze as a large rat scurried across his boot.

Martha **doesn't** think they'll win. (*Not,* **don't**—see page 11.)

The question mark, exclamation point, and dash go outside the quotation marks when they refer to the whole sentence.

"..."?   "..."!   "..."—

Question mark outside a complete sentence:

Right
Did Woody Guthrie write the song "This Land Is My Land"?

Wrong
Did Woody Guthrie write the song "This Land Is My Land?"

Why? The whole sentence is a question. Place the question mark outside the end quotation mark.

Exclamation point outside a complete sentence:

Do an immediate backup with "Safe-Save"!

Dash outside a complete sentence:

The guard growled, "Move it!"—I figured he meant me.

Use single quotation marks (' ') for quoted material inside a quotation.

"I'm hoping you'll say 'I do,' " said Michael.

"Dustin said, 'No way!' when I asked to borrow his Ferrari," Suzanne grumped.

DENNIS THE MENACE by Hank Ketcham

"HE SAID 'HOP IN THE CANOE,' SO I DID!"

Joe and they are friends. (*Not,* **Joe and them**—see page 21.)

APOSTROPHES

RED BASSET by Alex Graham

Use apostrophes ('):

▶ To take the place of an omitted letter or letters in a contraction. (When "not" becomes "n't," an apostrophe replaces the "o.")

do not = don't	should not = shouldn't
did not = didn't	would not = wouldn't
is not = isn't	cannot = can't
	(cannot, *not* can not)

Pete **can't** and **won't** give up his Reese's Pieces.
  (cannot)   *(will not)*

The apostrophe can also take the place of other letters:

who is = who's	you have = you've
who has = who's	there is = there's
it is = it's	she would = she'd
you are = you're	we will = we'll

Some contractions are easily confused with possessives:

Right
You're buying that car? **It's** a junker!

Wrong
Your buying that car? **Its** a junker!

? **Why?** *You're* and *it's* are contractions meaning "you are" and "it is." *Your* and *its* show possession. Remember, possessive *its* never sp**lits**. (See page 82.)

Sonia **dragged** the canoe onshore. (*Not,* **drug**—see page 96.)

Use apostrophes:

▸ To take the place of omitted numerals or letters.

Courtney's license expires in '02.
(2002)

The movie "Singin' in the Rain" made Gene Kelly famous.

▸ To form plurals of lowercase letters and abbreviations using capital letters with periods. Use the apostrophe if the meaning would be unclear without it. Leaving out the apostrophe for plurals of combinations of capital letters is gaining ground. (No apostrophe is needed to pluralize proper names.)

Here the meaning is unclear without an apostrophe to pluralize:

p's and q's   Ph.D.'s   S.O.S.'s

Moana got straight A's. (Would spell "As")

Tic-Tac-Toe uses O's and X's. (Would spell "Os")

Here the meaning is clear without an apostrophe to pluralize:

Stanton collected IOUs.

YWCAs   ABCs   CPUs   URLs

Carol knows many Marys.

the Grammys (awards)

the Wiggintons

▸ To form plurals of numbers (optional).

1900's *or* 1900s

All number 10's [10s], please step forward.

▸ To show possession. Apostrophes show ownership. The spelling depends on whether or not a word ends with *s*. Do the Two-Step Tango (next page) to figure out where to place those pesky apostrophes.

Carl Lewis went for the gold **medal**. (*Not*, **metal**—see page 65.)

Two-Step Tango
(for making words possessive)

Step 1: Decide if the word is singular or plural.

Step 2: Put **'s** or **'** at the end of the word, using these rules:

- If singular, add **'s**.
- If plural not ending in **s**, add **'s**.
- If plural ending in **s**, add **'** after the **s**.

Possession with Singular Words

If a word is singular, just add **'s**.

> President Thizzleberry**'s** banana split is melting.

Many people get confused when a singular noun ends in **s**. In these cases, however, you follow the same rules as with other singular nouns: add **'s**.

> Jesse Owens**'s** medals   Mother Jones**'s** march

Possession with Plural Words

If the word is plural and doesn't end in **s**, add **'s**.

> Lines for men**'s** bathrooms move faster than for women**'s**.
> *(plural)*   *(plural)*

If the word is plural and ends in **s**, just add **'** after the **s**.

> The Rolling Stones**'** Chicago concert was a media event.
> *(plural)*

Possession with Plural Compound Nouns

With compound nouns, first make the important word plural. Then add **'s** at the end of the word.

Singular	Step 1–Plural	Step 2–Plural Possessive
attorney-at-law	attorneys-at-law	attorneys-at-law**'s**
passerby	passersby	passersby**'s**
son-in-law	sons-in-law	sons-in-law**'s**

Stevie Wonder sang "Isn't She **Lovely?**" (*Not,* **Lovely**"?—see page 58.)

TIP: Like "commander in chief," "editor in chief" has no hyphens.

The editors in chief**'s** conference was slated for Trinidad.
(pluralize "editors")

HYPHENS

Use hyphens (**-**) :

▸ With prefixes (such as *ex-*, *quasi-*, *self-*) or when the root word is capitalized. (See page 68.)

    ex-jock   self-serve   mid-December

▸ With hyphenated names.

    Bailey-Wolff   Somerset-Wilson

▸ With compound numbers from 21 to 99 and with written fractions. (For more about numbers, see page 92.)

    thirty-two   five-eighths   seven and three-quarters

▸ With numbers to show age.

    three-year-old child   11- to 14-year-old swimmers

▸ With compound adjectives *before* a noun. (Compound adjectives consist of two or more words that work together to describe a noun. Together, they express a single thought.) Do not use hyphens when compound modifiers follow the noun. (See page 35.)

    six-foot-two athlete, *but* The athlete was **six foot two**.

    G-flat-minor piece, *but* Play something in **G flat minor**.

    African-American woman, *but* She was an **African American**.

▸ To show where words divide by syllables at the end of a line. (Today, with word processors and typesetting, hyphens are used much less frequently to show word division. Check a dictionary for division by syllables.)

Have lunch **with Catherine and me.** (*Not,* **Catherine and I**—see page 19.)

QUESTION MARKS

Use a question mark (**?**):

▸ When a sentence asks a direct question.

Who won the World Series?

▸ For a series of questions within the same sentence.

What spaghetti sauce do you want? marinara? meat? clam?

(Note: The questions are all within the same sentence. Don't capitalize the sauce names.)

▸ To suggest uncertainty.

Tubby said he ate three (?) rhubarb pies.

▸ With a question within a sentence.

Did I forget deodorant? wondered Sylvester.

▸ Inside parentheses if a question is asked.

Chris's pancakes (when did *he* learn to cook?) were superb.

(Note: This parenthetical question appears inside another sentence. Don't use a capital letter on "when.")

Do not use a question mark when a sentence asks an indirect question. The sentences below are both declarative.

I wonder if Bill still likes Hostess cupcakes.

Christina asked Jorge if he'd checked the stock prices.

Bob's the **best** climber of the three. (*Not,* **better**—see page 39.)

EXCLAMATION POINTS

ZITS by Jerry Scott and Jim Borgman

Like an alarm clock, an exclamation point wakes up your reader.

Use an exclamation point:

▶ To show strong emotion or surprise.

I refuse to pick up cow plops**!**

▶ To emphasize words.

"California or Bust**!**" read the sign on the covered wagon.

▶ To give an order.

"Give me back my teeth**!**" yelled Bucky.

Don't overdo exclamation points—use only one.

"No noodles**!**" yelled Donna.
not
"No noodles**!!!!**" yelled Donna.

Do not use a comma or a period after an exclamation point.

On **1 January 2000,** computers may go haywire. (*Not,* **1, January,** 2000—see page ▸

64

PART IV:
WORD POWER

"I" before "e" or "e" before "i"? To capitalize or not to capitalize? "Different from" or "different than"?

This next section spotlights language's finer points—the words themselves. Take spelling, for instance. How do you look up a word in the dictionary if you're not sure how to spell it? Let misspeller's dictionaries and spellcheckers come to the rescue. Unless you're a spelling ace, you probably have your own spelling demons: scissors? occcasional? cantaloupe? prescription? weird? You'll find some easy spelling rules and learn how to work around your personal spelling bugaboos.

Rules also help with knowing when to use capital letters—it's "Aunt Ruth," but "Ruth is my aunt." It's "President Jimmy Carter," but "Jimmy Carter, the president."

Pronunciation holds the key to spelling some words. When a sports commentator says, "He's a fine ath-uh-lete," you wonder if the word's spelled "athelete," or "athlete." (It's athlete!)

Then there are the copycats—confusing words that either sound or look alike. Other easy mix-ups offer close-but-no-cigar pitfalls, such as an Olympic gold medal and the precious metal gold. Learning the differences will help you know why "This tastes good" is right, but "You did good" is wrong.

Never fear. Words can be fun. Bad spelling is not an indication of intelligence. Easy mix-ups and copycats *can* be conquered. You *can* say "nuclear" correctly. With a little careful attention, you'll ease right through these sticky wickets.

ie's world cruise is planned for **October 2007**. (*Not*, **October, 2007**—see page 89.)

Spelling

SALLY FORTH by Greg Howard

First, let's look at the basics. Learn these easy spelling rules:

1. Use *i* before *e* except after *c*, or when the letters sound like *a*, as in "neighbor" or "weigh."

    i before e: believe, field, yield, fiend
    e follows c: receive, ceiling
    sounding like a: rein, lei, deign, skein

2. When two vowels go walking, the first one does the talking. When two vowels appear side by side, say the long vowel sound of the first. The second vowel of the pair is silent.

    boat   clean   roam   wait   steam   fries

3. Possessive *its* never splits. (See page 82.)

    Possessive: The dog wagged **its** tail.
    Contraction for "it is":   **It's** a pie-eating contest.

4. To change most nouns ending with *e* to adjectives, cross off the *e* and add a **y**.

    ice/icy   smoke/smoky   sponge/spongy
    scare/scary   spike/spiky   stone/stony

Enid, please **lend** me that grammar book. (*Not*, **loan**—see page 82.)

NOUN PLURALS

B.C. by Johnny Hart

Most nouns, including those that end in a vowel followed by a **y**, form the plural by adding **s**.

    birds   boys   cars   dudes   monkeys

To make words plural when they end in a consonant followed by a **y**, change the **y** to **i** and add **es**.

    penny/pennies   sky/skies   story/stories

Words ending in **s**, **ss**, **x**, **o**, **ch**, and **sh** form the plural by adding **es**.

    box**es**   gas**es**
    bush**es**   kiss**es**
    church**es**   tomato**es**, potato**es**, hero**es**

For musical words ending in **o,** simply add **s.**

    alto/alto**s**   cello/cello**s**   piano/piano**s**   soprano/soprano**s**

For nouns ending in **f** or **fe**, change the **f** or **fe** to **v** and add **es**.

    loaf/loa**ves**   calf/cal**ves**   knife/kni**ves**   life/li**ves**

Some words stay the same, whether singular or plural.

    sheep/sheep   deer/deer   moose/moose   trousers/trousers

Other words have different spellings in the plural form.

    child/children goose/geese medium/media tooth/teeth
    foot/feet   man/men   mouse/mice   woman/women

We **haven't gone** over that yet, Patty. (*Not,* **haven't went**—see page 10.)

PREFIXES AND SUFFIXES

B. C. by Johnny Hart

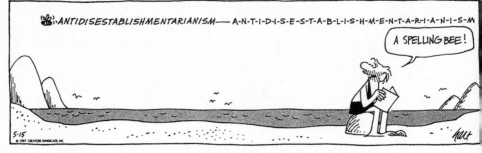

Adding Prefixes

Prefixes are beginning word parts. Put them in front of main words to change meaning:

anti- + war = antiwar	non- + essential = nonessential
mid- + term = midterm	pre- + view = preview
multi- + purpose = multipurpose	re- + union = reunion

TIP: With most words, the spelling of both the prefix and the main word stays the same.

Some prefixes need a hyphen to show a different meaning.

"Recount" means "tell a tale."
"Re-count" means "count again."

Many words that once were spelled with a hyphen now have no hyphen. Some have become one word; others have become two separate words. For example, "non-fiction" has become "nonfiction"; "income-tax" has become "income tax." If in doubt, check a dictionary.

Adding Suffixes

Suffixes are ending word parts. Put them at the end of main words to change meaning. Here are some suffixes:

-able -ance -ed -ing -less -ly -ment -ous -self -ful

TIP: The only word that ends with "full" is "full." All other words ending in the suffix *ful*, such as "helpful" and "wonderful," have only one *l*.

Nancy caught the **principal** culprits. (*Not*, **principle**—see page 84.)

When suffixes are added to root words (the simple base of a word), they form new words, such as charm**ing**, clue**less**, enjoy**ment**.

TIP: If a suffix begins with a consonant, the spelling of most main words stays the same.

> amaze + ment = amazement
> dark + ness = darkness
> slow + ly = slowly

If a suffix begins with a vowel and the main word ends with *e*, drop the *e*, then add the suffix.

> dance + ing = dancing include + ed = included
> glide + ing = gliding store + ing = storing
> hope + ed = hoped write + ing = writing

When a word ends in a consonant followed by a **y**, change the **y** to *i*, and then add the suffix.

> dr**y** + ed = dried marr**y** + age = marriage
> eas**y** + ly = easily merr**y** + est = merriest

When a word ends in **y**, change the **y** to *i*, and then add the suffix.

> hurry/hurr**ies**/hurr**ied** study/stud**ies**/stud**ied**
> query/quer**ies**/quer**ied** try/tr**ies**/tr**ied**

With one-syllable words ending in a single consonant with a vowel before it, double the consonant and add the suffix.

> beg/beg**ged** run/run**ning**
> hot/hot**ter** swim/swim**mer**

Olya raced **quickly** down the soccer field. (*Not*, **quick**—see page 36.)

OTHER SPELLING HURDLES

Words That Sound the Same

Some words sound the same but have different meanings. Confusing these sound-alikes (homonyms) can cause spelling errors—*boar/bore; there/they're/their; navel/naval; too/to/two; know/no; its/it's; whose/who's.* (See "Homonym Hash," pages 90–91, for more.)

THE FAMILY CIRCUS by Bil Keane

"Bundt cake? No thanks. I'd rather have a piece of home-run cake."

Ways to Tame the Spelling Monster

1. Keep a dictionary at hand.

2. Buy a misspeller's dictionary. Look up a word the way you think it *might* be spelled. Under that incorrect spelling you'll usually find the correct spelling.

3. Use a computer spellchecker. It will catch errors such as these: *develope, preperation, embarass,* and others. (Beware: Computers won't catch homonym goofs!) (See pages 90–91 for a list of homonyms.)

4. Keep a list of your own worst spelling monsters.

5. Use memory tricks to help with spelling:

   ▸ "Friend" ends in "end."

   ▸ "Desert" has one **s**—think **s**nake in the desert.
     "Dessert" has two **s**'s—think **s**trawberry **s**hortcake!

   ▸ "Stationery" (writing paper)—think of the **e** in **e**nvelope and l**e**tter.
     "Stationary" (unmoving)—think of the **a** in st**a**ble and st**a**nding.

   ▸ "Weird" doesn't fit the **i** before e rule. Say "**We** are **we**ird."

   ▸ "Necessary" has one **c** and two **s**'s.
     "Occasional" has two **c**'s and one **s**.

The **Guilfords** like to go camping. (*Not,* **Guilford's**—see page 60.)

Pronunciation

ABY BLUES by Rick Kirkman and Jerry Scott

Silent letters can make spelling hard.

the **c** in s**c**issors   the **p** in **p**neumonia
the **n** in hym**n**   the **k** in **k**not
the **t** in of**t**en   the **g** in **g**nat
the **p** in **p**sychology   the **th** in as**th**ma

Incorrect pronunciation can be good for a laugh:

chasm   Say, "ka´ sm," *not* "chasm" (as in "chair").

chic   Say, "sheek," *not* "chick." ("Chic" is a French word.)

colonel   Say, "ker´ nel," *not* "cah´ luh nul."

corps   Say, "core," *not* "corpse."

hyperbole Say, "high per´ buh lee," *not* "high´ per bowl."

Illinois   Say, "Il lih noy´," *not* "Il lih noise´."

respite   Say, "res´ pet," *not* "re spite´."

sword   Say, "sord," *not* "sword." (Don't pronounce the *w*.)

There are crazy things happening. (*Not,* **There's** [there is]—see page 11.)

SAY IT RIGHT! SPELL IT RIGHT!

Despite the tricky words on the previous page, saying words correctly can often help you spell them correctly. Check how you say these words. (Accented syllables are marked.)

👍 Right	👎 Wrong
Arc´ tic (**Ark´** tic)	~~Are´~~ tic
ask	~~ax~~
as´ ter **isk**	as´ te ~~rick~~
ath´ lete	a´ th~~uh~~ lete
es cape´ (ess cape´)	~~ex~~ cape´
et cet´ e ra (**et** ce´ te ra)	~~ect~~ cet´ e ra
length (lenkth)	~~lenth~~
nu´ **cle** ar (NOO **clee** er)	nu´ ~~cue~~ lar
pic´ ture (**PICK** ture)	~~pitch´~~ er
per spi ra´ tion	~~pre~~ spe ra´ tion
Re´**al** tor (REE al ter)	Re´ ~~luh~~ ter
sup po´se **dly**	sup po´ se ~~bly~~
Don't skip the "**r**" in these two:	
Feb´ ru ar y (Feb´ **roo** air y)	Feb´ ~~you~~ ar y
li´ brar y (lie´ **brair** ee)	li´ ~~berr~~ y

Thirty-year-old Bubbles LaRue wed Blake West. (*Not,* **Thirty year old**—see page 6

Speaking of Grammar! (Oral Errors)

Careful speech shows you're a pro. Avoid these easy-to-make errors.

Right	Wrong
"They **look like** gangsters." *or* "They **look as though** they're gangsters."	"They **look to be** gangsters."
"The **reason is** . . ." *or* "**Because** . . ."	"The **reason is because** . . ."
"**As far as the movie goes** (*or* **is concerned**), you choose." *or* "**As for the movie**, you choose."	"**As far as the movie**, you choose."
" . . . **with regard to** . . . "	" . . . **with regards to** . . . " (no *s*)
" . . . **in regard to** . . . "	" . . . **in regards to** . . ." (no *s*)
"The boss is **orienting** us to the new system."	"The boss is **orientating** us to the new system."
"I **graduated from** high school."	"I **graduated** high school." (needs "from")

It's perfect **for him** and Ruth Kay. (*Not,* **for he**—see page 19.)

👍 **Right**	👎 **Wrong**
"I **couldn't** care less." (It is not possible to care less than I care now.)	"I could care less." (I **could** care less than I care now.)
"That's **too high** a price."	"That's **too high of** a price." (no "of")
"I'll **try to** finish the test."	"I'll **try and** finish the test."
"And then he **says**, 'Great!' "	"And then he **goes**, 'Great!' "
"He **should have** called."	"He **should of** called."

TIP: Avoid oral fillers. Here are some of the worst offenders:

anyways	sort of
basically	totally
fully	uh
hopefully (See page 82.)	well
kind of	You know?
like	You know what I'm saying?

"Help!" yelled Harrison from the snake pit. (*Not*, **"Help!,"**—see page 64.)

Capitalization

To capitalize or not to capitalize? Just follow the rules.

Use a capital letter:

▶ For the pronoun "I."

▶ For all proper nouns. (See page 14 for the definition of a proper noun.)

▶ At the beginning of a sentence.

▶ At the beginning of quotations.

"Be mine, Olive Oyl," begged Popeye.

If a quotation is interrupted by a speaker, the second part of the quotation begins with a lowercase letter.

"Jonathan," Alison said sweetly, "we're out of film."

If a quotation is two separate sentences interrupted by a speaker, capitalize the first letter of the second sentence.

"That's it!" said Kiki. "You're history."

(Note: Put a period after "Kiki"—these are two complete sentences.)

▶ For names of specific people and things.

Michael Jordan   Dr. Seuss   London Bridge   Indian Ocean

▶ For days of the week, months, and holidays.

Wednesday   July   Thanksgiving

▶ For copyrighted names, brand names, and trademarks.

Nike	Wheaties	Lean Cuisine	QuarkXPress
Donald Duck	Kleenex	Levi's	Polo
Macintosh	Quicken	Harley-Davidson	

▶ For names of companies, organizations, and schools.

Eddie Bauer   Planned Parenthood   Northwestern University

The **ten-foot** fence didn't stop the opossum. (*Not*, The **ten foot**—see page 62.)

▸ For names of buildings, monuments, and parks.

Empire State Building   Lincoln Memorial   Central Park
(building)   *(monument)*   *(park)*

▸ For the first, last, and important words of titles of plays, books, television series, movies, poems, magazines, articles. (Do not capitalize prepositions; the articles *a*, *an*, or *the*; or conjunctions, unless they are used as the first or last word of a title.) (For italics versus quotation marks, see pages 56 and 92.)

Play:	*Death of a Salesman*
Book:	*The Cat in the Hat*
Television Series:	*ER*
Movie:	*Mr. Smith Goes to Washington*
Poem:	"Waiting at the Window"
Magazine:	*Scientific American*
Article:	"How to Weave the World Over"

▸ For names of places, languages, streets, cities, and states.

Place:	Shangri-la
Language:	Swahili
Street:	McMillan Road
City, State:	Duluth, Minnesota

▸ For geographical regions (but not directions).

Regions:	Southeast, Southern California, New England, Midwest
Directions:	north, south, east, west

▸ For names of important historical events, documents, and specific school subjects.

Event:	Vietnam War
Document:	Gettysburg Address
Specific Class:	Chemistry 101

When the subject is general, don't use a capital letter.

Norbert is clueless in chemistry.

TIP: Do not capitalize the seasons—summer, fall, winter, spring.

The **children's** room is a disaster. (*Not*, **childrens'**—see page 61.)

▶ Don't capitalize titles if they appear alone or after a name.

Secretary of the Treasury Martin Tightwad filed for bankruptcy.

Martin Tightwad, secretary of the treasury, filed for bankruptcy.
  (name)   *(title)*

The **secretary of the treasury** filed for bankruptcy.

▶ For titles used in place of names in direct address.

Welcome aboard, Captain.

▶ For the first word of a sentence or line of poetry.

"Two roads diverged in a yellow wood . . . " (Robert Frost)

▶ For each letter of an initial.

W. C. Fields   W. E. B. DuBois

▶ For naming relatives. If a possessive pronoun or article appears before a noun that indicates a relative, don't capitalize the noun. If the "relative" noun appears alone or with a name, capitalize it.

"I told **my father** I needed the car!" whined Freddie.
"I told **Father** I needed the car!" whined Freddie.

Jill talked to **her aunt**.
Jill talked to **Aunt Helen**.

Our grandmother loves in-line skating.
Grandma Bracken loves in-line skating.

Between you and me, I'm stoked. (*Not*, **Between you and I**—see page 19.)

Easy Mix-Ups

affect/effect

"Affect" is usually a verb, meaning "to influence."

> Jerry Seinfeld has *affected* the career plans of many young comedians.

> How you feel about TV *affects* your viewing habits.

"Effect" is usually a noun, meaning "result."

> The *effect* of the cockroach invasion was a deserted café.

Far less common, when "effect" is used as a verb, it means "bring about."

> Scottie Pippin's injury *effected* a change in the NBA schedule.

TIP: Say "We *affect* [verb] the *effect* [noun]."

anymore/any more

"Anymore," an adverb, means "now." Use it only at the end of a sentence to show a negative meaning.

> Chloë doesn't eat hot dogs *anymore*.
> > *not*
> Anymore, Chloë doesn't eat hot dogs.

(Substitute "nowadays": *Nowadays*, Chloë doesn't eat hot dogs.)

Use "any more" to emphasize something extra.

> Divine Doughnuts doesn't have *any more* cinnamon rolls.

a lot/alot

Use "a lot," *not* "alot." "Alot" is incorrect. Make it two words.

> R. J. can chow down *a lot* of nacho chips.

Lucy loves the **principle** of hard work. (*Not*, **principal**—see page 84.)

all ready/already

"All ready" means "all set."

> We are *all ready* for our island cruise.

"Already" means something has taken place.

> Tannika has *already* had the chicken pox.

all right/alright

Use "all right." "Alright" is incorrect. Make it two words.

> "I'm *all right!*" Sara yelled down from the helicopter.

all together/altogether

Use "all together" for "everyone at the same time" or "all in a group."

> "*All together* now—Surprise!" called Maria.

Use "altogether" to mean "completely," "all told," "wholly," "entirely."

> That show was *altogether* cheesy.

bad/badly

"Bad" is an adjective. It describes nouns or pronouns.

> Mrs. Scaponi did a *bad* job on the lasagna.

"Badly" is an adverb. It describes verbs and answers the question *how*.

> Tiger Woods played *badly* on the miniature golf course.
>   (verb) (adverb)

Important exception: Use "bad" with verbs of the five senses.

Sight:	Those fuzzy green leftovers *look bad.*
Touch:	The hot sand *feels bad* on Pepper's paws.
Hearing:	Your cough *sounds bad.*
Taste:	Garlic *tastes bad* to Louise.
Smell:	Our neighborhood skunk *smells bad.*

She and I hate elevator music. (*Not,* **Her and me**—see page 21.)

Also use "bad" with feelings:

> I *feel bad* about your accident.
> *not*
> I *feel badly* about your accident.

TIP: "I feel badly" means something has happened to your sense of touch or your fingers are numb.

bring/take

Use "bring" to mean "come toward." Use "take" to mean "go away from."

> "*Bring* me my dragon slippers." (The action is toward you.)
>
> "*Take* that monstrosity to the rummage sale." (The action is away from you.)

TIP: "Bring" is like "come," and "take" is like "go."

> "*Come* here."   "*Go* away."

can/may

"Can" means "is able to." "May" asks permission.

> Paul Newman *can* drive race cars.
>
> *May* I join him?

different from/different than

Things differ *from* one another. Use "different from" to compare. The only time "different than" should be used is when a clause follows it.

> New York City is *different from* Los Angeles.
>
> Today's music is much *different than* it was fifty years ago.
> *(clause)*

disinterested/uninterested

"Disinterested" means "neutral" or "objective." "Uninterested" means "lacking interest in."

> Judges want *disinterested* jurors, not *uninterested* jurors.

The young hunk ordered **dessert**. (*Not*, **desert**—see page 70.)

farther/further

There's a "far" in "farther." Use "farther" for physical distance.

Moscow is *farther* from Maryland than from London.

Use "further" to show "more" or "to a greater extent."

Vinny's smirk gave *further* proof of his betrayal.

fewer/less

Use "fewer" with things you can count: *fewer* marbles, *fewer* skyscrapers. Use "less" with things that can't be counted: *less* sense, *less* courage.

Sign at check-out counter: "*Fewer* than ten items."

Fewer than twenty people entered the hog-calling contest.

G. I. Joe has *less* sex appeal than Ken.

Also use "less" with time: *less* than three minutes.

good/well

"Good" is an adjective. It describes nouns or pronouns. "Well" is usually an adverb. It describes verbs and answers the question *how*.

Linnet makes *good* tamales.

Play practice went *well*.

Use "good" with verbs of the five senses.

Sight:	The Toe Tappers *looked good* in the talent show.
Touch:	Silk pajamas *feel good*.
Hearing:	Your tuba solo *sounded good*.
Taste:	Fish tacos *taste good*.
Smell:	Fresh lilacs *smell good*.

Also use "good" with feelings:

Now that the shoe fits, Cinderella *feels good*.

The Chicago Bulls won on **June 13, 1997**. (*Not*, **June 13 1997**—see page 89.)

Use "well" with health. It's the opposite of "sick."

> After eating Paco's Pepper Chili, Tina didn't *feel well.*
> *not*
> After eating Paco's Pepper Chili, Tina didn't *feel good.*

hopefully

"Hopefully," an adverb meaning "full of hope," has become a filler word. Banish "hopefully" when it has no verb to modify. Substitute "full of hope" to see if a sentence makes sense.

> *Hopefully,* the twins crept down the stairs Christmas morning.

When the twins *crept,* they were full of hope. Here, *hopefully* is correct.

> *Hopefully,* my phone will ring tonight."

A phone can't be filled with hope. Instead, say "I hope my phone will ring tonight."

its/it's

"Its" is a possessive pronoun. Remember, "Possessive *its* never spl*its*!"

> The burro flicked flies from *its* ears.

It's = it is

> *It's* even too expensive for Ted Turner.

lend/loan

"Lend" is a verb. "Loan" is a noun.

The verb "lend":

> **Present tense:** The Marine Bank *lends* money.
> **Past tense:**   I *lent* Holly my favorite book.

Never "*Loan* me five dollars" or "Cameron *loaned* me a pen."

The noun "loan":

> We took out a *loan.*

(Note: Although "loan" is creeping into use as a verb, we like the old rule, explained above. Use "lend" as a verb, "loan" as a noun.)

Every player washed **her** uniform. (*Not,* **their**—see page 20.)

lie/lay

It's easy to mix up the irregular verbs "lie" (to recline) and "lay" (to place). Note how "lay" shows up twice on the chart below. It is the past tense of "lie" and the present tense of "lay." No wonder it causes problems!

LIE The verb "lie" means "recline." It is not followed by a direct object. (A direct object answers the question *who* or *what*.)

You *lie* down today.
   (*verb*)   (*no object*)

You *lay* down yesterday.

You *had lain* down last week.

RUBES by Leigh Rubin

Contrary to popular belief,
not all dinosaurs were cold-blooded.

TIP: Say, "Let's go *lie* in the sun," *not* "Let's go *lay* in the sun." Use the present tense of *lie*.

Present	Past	Past Participle (needs a helping verb)
lie (*to recline; to rest horizontally*)	lay	lain
lay (*to place*)	laid	laid

LAY The verb "lay" means "set" or "place." "Lay" is followed by a direct object. (See page 44.)

You *lay* the hamburger on the plate today.
   (*verb*)   (*direct object*)

You *laid* the hamburger on the plate yesterday.

You *had laid* the hamburger on the plate last week.

Becky's smile **cheers** her patients. (*Not,* **cheer**—see page 8.)

TIP: The verb "lie" can also mean "fib." It follows a regular verb pattern:

I lie.   I lied.   I had lied.

The verb "lay" can also mean "to deposit," as in "The hen lays an egg." It also follows a regular pattern:

It lays.   It laid.   It had laid.

nauseous/nauseated

"Nauseous," an adjective, means "causing nausea or disgust." "Nauseated," a verb, means "to feel sick or disgusted." Don't say that you feel *nauseous*. That means you are making other people feel sick or disgusted! If you're unwell, you may feel *nauseated*.

TIP: These easy mix-ups, "nauseous" and "nauseated," are like "poisonous" and "poisoned." Even if your food's been poisoned, *you're* not poisonous, unless you're a deadly stonefish.

percent/percentage

Use "percent" with a number. Use "percentage" when a number is omitted.

Ninety *percent* of the rabbits reproduced.

What *percentage* of the tires went flat?

principal/principle

The adjective "principal" means "first in importance": a *principal* investigator. The noun "principal" means "main person or thing": the *principal's* your **pal**.

"Principal" also means "money": *principal* and interest.

Scrooge had to draw on the *principal* to repay the debt.

The noun "principle" means "fundamental truth" or "rule."

Murphy's Laws contain *principles* that never fail.

TIP: Both *principle* and *rule* end with **le**.

Where is Stewart? (*Not,* **Where's Stewart at?**—see page 33.)

regardless/irregardless

Regardless of what you may think, "irregardless," like "ain't," is not standard English.

than/then

Use the conjunction "than" for comparison when introducing a clause.

Antonio is taller *than* Stefan is.

Renny made more baskets *than* Matt did.

Use the adverb "then" to show time.

What happened *then*?

Emma swam and swam, *then* napped.

their/there/they're

"Their" is a possessive pronoun.

Their 1905 Cadillac has one cylinder.

"There" shows place and can also be used to begin a sentence.

There are awesome sports cars over *there*.

"They're" means "they are."

They're going to bronze Michael Jordan's shoes.

to/too/two

"To" helps form the infinitive of a verb: I wanted *to* shout. (See page 6.)

"Too" means also: We're going, *too*.

"Two" means the number "2": *Two* cats fought.

your/you're

"Your" is the possessive pronoun: "*Your* serve is awesome, Lindsay," *not* "*You're* serve is awesome, Lindsay."

"You're" stands for "you are"—"*You're* late," *not* "*Your* late."

These kinds of shoes pinch. (*Not,* **These kind**—see page 11.)

PART V:
APPENDIX

A

ABBREVIATIONS An abbreviation is a shortened form that stands for a word or group of words. Most take periods. A few don't.

e.g. The abbreviation "e.g." means "for example." Always put a comma before and after "e.g."

Bring one pirate prop, e.g., hook, sword, or patch.

et al. The abbreviation "et al." means "and others" and is used only in bibliographic entries and footnotes: Smith, George, et al.

etc. The abbreviation "etc." stands for *et cetera*. It means "and so forth." Put a comma before "etc."

We'll play Monopoly, Scrabble, Uno, etc.

ff. The abbreviation "ff." means "and the following pages."

ibid. The abbreviation "ibid." means "in the same book or passage." It is used in bibliographic entries and footnotes when an entry is from the same source as the previous one.

i.e. The abbreviation "i.e." means "that is." Use "i.e." for explanations. Always put a comma before and after "i.e."

I saw a gaberlunzie, i.e., a wandering beggar.

M.D. *or* **MD** "M.D." stands for Doctor of Medicine.

Ms. The abbreviation "Ms." is commonly used before a woman's name instead of "Miss" or "Mrs." Like "Mr.," "Ms." does not indicate marital status.

Mary Kay wrote the book's **foreword**. (*Not,* **forward**—see page 90.)

86

PS The abbreviation "PS" stands for *postscript*. (Note: Use no periods.)

 PS I love you.

R.S.V.P. *or* **RSVP** The abbreviation R.S.V.P. stands for *répondez s'il vous plaît*. It means "please respond," or, literally, "respond, if you please."

State Abbreviations The United States Post Office uses two-letter abbreviations for all fifty states. (Note: no periods.)

AL	Alabama	LA	Louisiana	OH	Ohio
AK	Alaska	ME	Maine	OK	Oklahoma
AR	Arkansas	MD	Maryland	OR	Oregon
AZ	Arizona	MA	Massachusetts	PA	Pennsylvania
CA	California	MI	Michigan	RI	Rhode Island
CO	Colorado	MN	Minnesota	SC	South Carolina
CT	Connecticut	MO	Missouri	SD	South Dakota
DE	Delaware	MS	Mississippi	TN	Tennessee
FL	Florida	MT	Montana	TX	Texas
GA	Georgia	NE	Nebraska	UT	Utah
HI	Hawaii	NC	North Carolina	VA	Virginia
ID	Idaho	ND	North Dakota	VT	Vermont
IL	Illinois	NH	New Hampshire	WA	Washington
IN	Indiana	NJ	New Jersey	WV	West Virginia
IA	Iowa	NM	New Mexico	WI	Wisconsin
KS	Kansas	NV	Nevada	WY	Wyoming
KY	Kentucky	NY	New York		

ARTICLES The articles "the," "a," and "an" signal that a noun is coming.

"The" is a *definite article*. Use "the" for a specific noun.

 the party the football

"A" and "an" are *indefinite articles*. Use "a" before words that start with a consonant sound.

 a mouse a cow

Use "an" with words that start with a vowel sound.

 an artichoke an umbrella

"A" and "the" with the word *number*: The verb that follows the word *number* may be singular or plural. It depends on whether you use "a" or "the."

The giraffe scratched **its** neck. (*Not*, **it's**—see pages 20 and 82.)

When the article "the" appears before "number," use a singular verb. Think of the members of a group acting as one unit.

> **The number** of ants in the kitchen **is** increasing.
> [Implied: "It" is increasing.]

When the article "a" appears before "number," use a plural verb. Think of individual members of a group fanning out like ants on the march.

> **A number** of ants **are** swarming into the kitchen.
> [Implied: "They" are swarming.]

B

BRACKETS Use brackets to indicate information that isn't part of the original material.

> "I found diaries from the Civil War [1861–1865]," Frazier said.

Enclose the term "*sic*," meaning "just as it was written," in brackets. "*Sic*" means that something has been faithfully reproduced from the original, even if the original was wrong.

> He doesn't live here no [*sic*] more.

> Livingston wrote, "We saw a desert oiasis [*sic*]."

C

COMMAS A comma usually comes before titles such as Ph.D. or CPA (Certified Public Accountant).

> Kirsten E. Josephson, Ph.D.
> Shirley Springer, D.D.S.

Sources differ on Jr. and Sr. Some prefer the use of commas, while others prefer no commas. Whatever you choose, be consistent.

> Martin Luther King, Jr.   Martin Luther King Jr.

D

DASHES With most word processors you can make "em" (—) and "en" (–) dashes. Use em dashes with phrases in sentences. For example, "You brought See's chocolates—my favorite." (See page 55 for more on dashes.)

The seals were all **lying** on their backs. (*Not*, **laying**—see pages 83–84.)

The em dash (—) is the width of the letter *m*. Use it with words, not numbers.

> They grabbed the slipping wedding cake—too late!

The en dash (–) is the width of the letter *n*. Use it with numbers as a minus sign, with ranges, and between dates:

> 14 – 6 = 8
> San Diego's temperatures average 40°– 80° Fahrenheit.
> pages 159–229
> The Civil War, 1861–1865
> 11 P.M.–1 P.M.

DATES When a month comes before a year, no comma is needed.

> The cows rioted in July 1997.

When a date includes month, day, and year, use commas between the day and the year and between the year and the rest of the sentence.

> We met on November 15, 1996, and married two years later.

If the day appears before the month, no commas are needed. Sometimes in business or the military, and in other countries, dates are presented this way:

> Complete the Hansen Project by 9 June 2002.

E

ELLIPSES Ellipses are periods with spaces in between. Use three dots to take the place of omitted words within a quoted sentence.

> At age 100, labor leader Mother Jones said, "I'm just an old war horse . . . ready for battle . . . but too worn out to move."

If the omitted words follow a complete sentence, use four dots—a period plus the three dots of ellipses.

> "Dorothy caught Toto at last and started to follow her aunt. . . .
> The house whirled around two or three times and rose slowly
> through the air."
> —*The Wizard of Oz*, L. Frank Baum

"I'll **help**," said Gina. (*Not*, **help**",—see page 56.)

H

I NEED HELP by Vic Lee

HOMONYM HASH Homonyms are words that sound alike but have different meanings and spellings. Here are a few:

aid *(to help; help)*	aide *(assistant)*
altar *(for worship)*	alter *(to change)*
bare *(naked)*	bear *(animal; to carry)*
bore *(drill a hole; make weary by being dull)*	boar *(wild pig)*
bundt *(fancy baking pan)*	bunt *(to bat lightly)*
buy *(to purchase)*	by *(preposition)*
capital *(seat of government)*	capitol *(government building)*
cite *(to refer to)* sight *(vision)*	site *(place)*
creak *(sound)*	creek *(water)*
dear *(beloved)*	deer *(animal)*
fair *(honest; carnival)*	fare *(fee)*
for *(preposition)* fore *(in front of)*	four *(number)*
foreword *(book preface)*	forward *(toward the front)*
fowl *(bird)*	foul *(dirty, rotten)*
frees *(sets at liberty)*	freeze *(to turn into ice)*
hear *(to listen to)*	here *(place)*
let's *(meaning "let us")*	lets *(allows; releases)*
naval *(related to ships or a navy)*	navel *(belly button)*
one *(1)*	won *(to have gained victory)*
pair *(two similar things)*	pare *(to scrape or cut back)*

Sophia **graduated** from college. (*Not*, **graduated** college—see page 73.)

peek *(to glimpse or see)* peak *(top, high point)*	pique *(to arouse interest in)*
plain *(simple)*	plane *(flying machine)*
sea *(ocean)*	see *(to view)*
seam *(the joining of two pieces)*	seem *(to appear)*
serf *(slave)*	surf *(to ride waves on a board)*
sew *(to fasten with stitches)* so *(conjunction)*	sow *(to plant)*
something *(unspecified thing)*	some thing *(some object)*
stair *(step)*	stare *(to gaze)*
tea *(drink made with tea leaves)*	tee *(golf peg)*
team *(group)*	teem *(to swarm)*
their *(belonging to them)* they're *(they are)*	there *(place)*
threw *(released)*	through *(preposition)*
to *(preposition)* two *(number)*	too *(also)*
waist *(body part)*	waste *(garbage)*
wares *(goods)*	wears *(puts on)*
your *(belonging to you)*	you're *(you are)*

PEANUTS by Charles M. Schulz

I

ITALICS Use italics to emphasize.

I will *never* eat pink tofu again.

Also use italics for foreign words, unless they have become common (such as vis-à-vis):

fait accompli (French, meaning, "a done deal," or, literally, "deed accomplished.")

Molly and Peter **are** two impetuous kids. (*Not,* **is**—see page 16.)

Titles of magazines, newspapers, books, long poems, movies, plays, television series, musical works, and names of ships should be in italics.

> *Newsweek, The New York Times, Cold Mountain, Wreck of the Hesperus, The Sound of Music, Romeo and Juliet, Gunsmoke, Appalachian Spring, Star of India*

L

LINKING VERBS Linking verbs connect subjects with words or phrases in the predicate. Unlike helping verbs (see page 5), linking verbs can stand alone.

Common linking verbs: *be, am, is, was, were, become, seem, appear, believe, grow, remain, prove*.

> You *seem* tired.
>
> Shaquille *remains* popular.

Verbs for the five senses also are linking verbs: *look, feel, sound, taste, smell*.

> **Sight:** The Range Rover *looked* muddy.
> **Touch:** The kitten *felt* soft.
> **Hearing:** The whippoorwill *sounded* far away.
> **Taste:** The cabbage soup *tastes* terrible.
> **Smell:** Your sneakers *smell* funny.

For more about verbs, see pages 5–13.

N

NUMBERS Some sources say to spell out numbers from one to nine and to use figures above nine. Other sources say to spell out numbers from one to ninety-nine. Whichever rule you follow, be consistent.

> Jason ate thirty-one oatmeal cookies.
>
> As soon as she turned sixteen, Kay got her driver's license.
>
> The United States has fifty states.

All sources agree that if a sentence contains many numbers, you should use figures for them. If a number begins a sentence, write out the number or reword the sentence. For scientific or technical writing, use figures:

> Imelda Marcos had 2,350 pairs of shoes, 345 ball gowns, and 789 hats.
>
> Five hundred people attended the pep rally.
>
> Add 28.6 g of sucrose to 100 g of milk.

Theo was so full he **could hardly** finish. (*Not*, **couldn't hardly**—see page 37.)

P

POSSESSION If referring to one thing owned by two people, use the possessive only with the second person's name.

Carl and Sandra's car (They both own one car.)

If referring to things owned by separate people, use the possessive with both (or all) names.

Carl's and Sandra's cars (They own separate cars.)

PREPOSITIONS Do yourself a favor: Memorize the prepositions. That way, you'll never wonder which pronoun to use (I or me?, he or him?, etc.). Being able to spot prepositions will help you choose the objective form of pronouns to go with prepositional phrases: "from her and him," *not* "from she and he."

about	beneath	into	through
above	beside	like	throughout
across	between	near	to
after	beyond	of	toward
against	by	off	under
along	despite	on	underneath
among	down	onto	until
around	during	out	up
as	except	outside	upon
at	for	over	with
before	from	past	within
behind	in	regarding	without
below	inside	since	

Certain words take certain prepositions. For instance, capable *of*, basis *of* or *for*, affinity *for*, together *with*, agree *with*, on behalf *of*, belong *to*, outside/inside *of*, separate *from*, write *to*, parallel *to* or *with*, extract *from*, and expert *in*, *at*, or *with*. Say, "bragged about, *not* "bragged on."

PRONOUNS There are many types of pronouns. Here are a few more pronoun nuggets:

Indefinite Pronouns Indefinite pronouns refer to persons, places, or things in general. They can be singular or plural. (See pages 25–26.)

A **team** of pickpockets **was** nabbed yesterday. (*Not,* **team** . . . **were**—see page 15.)

TIP: Two subjects joined by "and" are considered singular if modified by "every," an indefinite pronoun. Say, "Every person gives."

Every man and woman on our block **gives** blood.
(indefinite pronoun)   *(third person singular verb)*

Demonstrative Pronouns Demonstrative pronouns point to specific persons, places, or things: *this, these, that, those*.

This cream puff is mine.   **That** is yours.   **Those** politicians!

Interrogative Pronouns Interrogative pronouns ask questions: *what, which, who, whom, whose*.

S

SUBJUNCTIVE MOOD Some sentences suggest an idea that is doubtful, contrary to the fact, or merely a wish or dream. With such "iffy" statements, use the subjunctive verb form "were" instead of "was." The words "if," "as if," and "as though" signal the subjunctive mood. So do "would" and "should."

PEANUTS by Charles M. Schulz

If I **were** Barbra Streisand, I'd sing at the White House. (I'm not Streisand.)

If Dad **were** to win the lottery, he'd quit his job. (Dad hasn't won yet!)

Blossom wishes she **were** younger. (Blossom will never be younger.)

Would that Don had booked another cruise! (Don hasn't booked another cruise.)

You've **piqued** my interest, Jan. (*Not,* **peeked** or **peaked**—see page 91.)

Exception: When a statement begins with "if," but is true, don't use the subjunctive mood.

If I **was** wrong, I apologize.

T

TIME Write out "time" words such as "midnight," "noon," or numbers on the hour, half hour, or quarter hour.

Vampires come out at **midnight**.

Beau and Hope embraced by the Eiffel Tower at **nine o'clock**.

When writing a specific time, use numerals. The abbreviation "A.M." means from midnight to noon. "P.M." means from noon to midnight. Use small capital letters for A.M. and P.M. If small capital letters are not an option on your computer, use either lowercase ("a.m." and "p.m.") or uppercase ("A.M." and "P.M.")

The train leaves at 8:37 A.M.

Court will adjourn at 5:15 P.M.

Do not combine A.M. or P.M. with words that indicate time, such as "morning" or "evening." (Don't say, "4:40 P.M. in the afternoon," for example.)

V

VERB FORMS (See pages 5–13 and 92 for more about verbs.) Some verbs are regular. Other verbs are irregular and don't follow the usual pattern. Here are some irregular verb forms:

Present	Past (no helping verb)	Past Participle (needs helping verb)
bear (*as in "carry"*)	bore	borne
begin	began	begun
bend	bent	bent
bite	bit	bitten
break	broke	broken
bring	brought (*never "brang"*)	brought (*never "brang"*)
catch	caught	caught
choose	chose	chosen
deal	dealt	dealt
dig	dug	dug
dive	dived (*dove*)	dived

I **definitely plan to visit** Speeder. (*Not*, **plan to definitely visit**—see page 6.)

Present	Past (no helping verb)	Past Participle (needs helping verb)
do	did	done
drag	dragged (*never "drug"*)	dragged (*never "drug"*)
drink	drank	drunk
fall	fell	fallen
feel	felt	felt
fly	flew	flown
forget	forgot	forgotten
freeze	froze	frozen
get	got	got, gotten
give	gave	given
go	went	gone
grow	grew	grown
hang (*suspend*)	hung	hung
hang (*execute*)	hanged	hanged
have	had	had
keep	kept	kept
lay	laid	laid
lend	lent	lent
lie (*recline*)	lay	lain
lie (*be untruthful*)	lied	lied
light	lighted, lit	lighted, lit
ring	rang	rung
ride	rode	ridden
run	ran	run
see	saw	seen
shine	shone	shone
shrink	shrank (*shrunk*)	shrunk (*shrunken*)
sing	sang	sung
sit	sat	sat
sneak	sneaked (*never "snuck"*)	sneaked (*never "snuck"*)
speak	spoke	spoken
steal	stole	stolen
stink	stank (*stunk*)	stunk
swim	swam	swum
take	took	taken
wear	wore	worn
weave	wove	woven
write	wrote	written

The team played **well**. (*Not,* **good**—see page 81.)

MORE GRAMMAR RESOURCES

Here are some of our favorite grammar books. Along with a good dictionary, keep several grammar guides on hand.

Baugh, L. Sue. *Essentials of English Grammar*. Lincolnwood, IL: NTC Publishing Group, 1995.

Furnish, Bob. *Write Right*. Bloomington, IN: Phi Delta Kappa, 1996.

Gibaldi, Joseph. *MLA Handbook for Writers of Research Papers*, 4th ed. New York: Modern Language Association of America, 1995.

Gordon, Karen Elizabeth. *The Deluxe Transitive Vampire: The Ultimate Handbook of Grammar for the Innocent, the Eager, & the Doomed*. New York: Pantheon Books, 1993.

————. *The New Well-Tempered Sentence: A Punctuation Handbook for the Innocent, the Eager, & the Doomed*. New York: Ticknor & Fields, 1993.

————. *Torn Wings and Faux Pas: A Flashbook of Style, A Beastly Guide Through the Writer's Labyrinth*. New York: Pantheon Books, 1997.

Kipfer, Barbara A., ed. by the Princeton Language Institute Staff. *Twenty-First Century Grammar Handbook*. New York: Dell, 1993.

Lederer, Richard and Dowis, Richard. *The Write Way: The S.P.E.L.L. Guide to Real-Life Writing*. New York: Pocket Books, 1995.

New World Dictionary Editors. *Webster's New World Misspeller's Dictionary*. New York: Macmillan General Reference, 1997.

O'Conner, Patricia T. *Woe Is I: The Grammarphobe's Guide to Better English in Plain English*. New York: Putnam Publishing Group, 1996.

Publication Manual of the American Psychological Association, 4th ed. (known as the *APA Manual*). Washington, D.C.: American Psychological Association, 1994.

Sabin, William A. *The Gregg Reference Manual*, 8th ed. Westerville, OH: Glencoe, 1996.

Strunk, William and White, E. B. *The Elements of Style*. Needham Heights, MA: Allyn & Bacon, 1995.

Webb, Suzanne. *Harbrace College Handbook*, 13th ed. San Diego: HBJ College & School Division, 1997.

Photo by Bob Bretell

"Grammar is a *very* serious business."
—The Grammar Patrol

Since 1985, Edith Fine (right) and Judith Josephson (left) have taught grammar and writing with a comic twist in their popular seminars. This dynamic duo is always on the lookout for bloopers and other sticky wickets in our ever-evolving language.

Fine and Josephson have written fiction and nonfiction for children and adults. Edith, a rabid recycler, loves long walks, classical music, and her Groucho glasses. She is the author of *Barbara McClintock, Nobel Prize Geneticist,* and other children's books. Judith, an avid swimmer, enjoys playing the violin in a community orchestra and writing biographies and poetry. She is the author of *Allan Pinkerton, The Original Private Eye; Mother Jones, Fierce Fighter for Workers' Rights; Jesse Owens, Track and Field Legend; Umbrellas,* and other children's books. With Pat Dorff, Edith and Judith are the authors of *File . . . Don't Pile!® For People Who Write.*

Fine and Josephson both love to get lost in good books. They live with their families in Encinitas, California.

INDEX